RUDOLF STEINER (1861–1925) called his spiritual philosophy 'anthroposophy', meaning 'wisdom of the human being'. As a highly developed seer, he based his work on direct knowledge and perception of spiritual dimensions. He initiated a modern and universal 'science of spirit', accessible to anyone willing to exercise clear and unprejudiced thinking.

From his spiritual investigations Steiner provided suggestions for the renewal of many activities, including education (both general and special), agriculture, medicine, economics, architecture, science, philosophy, religion and the arts. Today there are thousands of schools, clinics, farms and other organizations involved in practical work based on his principles. His many published works feature his research into the spiritual nature of the human being, the evolution of the world and humanity, and methods of personal development. Steiner wrote some 30 books and delivered over 6000 lectures across Europe. In 1924 he founded the General Anthroposophical Society, which today has branches throughout the world.

HEART THINKING
Inspired Knowledge

RUDOLF STEINER

Selected and compiled by Martina Maria Sam

RUDOLF STEINER PRESS

Translated by Matthew Barton

Rudolf Steiner Press,
Hillside House, The Square
Forest Row, RH18 5ES

www.rudolfsteinerpress.com

Published by Rudolf Steiner Press 2017

Originally published in German under the title *Herzdenken, Über inspiratives Erkennen* by Futurum Verlag, Basel, in 2014

© Futurum Verlag 2014
This translation © Rudolf Steiner Press 2017

A catalogue record for this book is available from the British Library

Print book ISBN: 978 1 85584 535 0
Ebook ISBN: 978 1 85584 493 3

Cover by Morgan Creative
Typeset by DP Photosetting, Neath, West Glamorgan
Printed and bound by 4Edge Ltd., Essex

Contents

Introduction

Anthroposophical works often refer to 'heart thinking' or 'thinking with the heart' as an important capacity which we need to develop in the modern world. In fact this expression only figures explicitly in a single lecture cycle—*Macrocosm and Microcosm*—which Rudolf Steiner gave in 1910.[1]

However, these lectures can help us recognize the intrinsic nature of heart thinking, and the quest to develop it, in other lectures and writings by Steiner. By compiling diverse aspects related to the theme, this little book seeks to illustrate what capacities exactly Rudolf Steiner was referring to when he coined the term 'heart thinking'.

In the series *Macrocosm and Microcosm* he offers exercises by means of which we can develop this thinking with the heart. They awaken in us a direct sense of truth which is indispensable in spiritual experience; and this is because we can only verify the imaginative perceptions we gain if we can distinguish between true and false pictures.[2]

It is not hard to discern in the inner gesture of these exercises the qualities Rudolf Steiner describes as 'virtues' or 'soul habits' in his key books on inner development, *Knowledge of the Higher Worlds* (1904, GA 10) and *The Stages of Higher Knowledge* (1905–8, GA 12). Comparing these and other texts we find that heart thinking can develop primarily through exercises given to acquire the faculty of Inspiration. Only when feeling undergoes a fundamental transformation through such exercises—that is, when it largely sheds its

personal and subjective character—can the heart become a
new organ of thinking.

Of numerous comments by Rudolf Steiner on this theme,
we therefore primarily selected for this anthology texts that
can offer an overview of exercises suited to developing
inspired knowledge, and thus 'heart thinking'. At the end of
this introduction I will briefly consider what common inner
gesture all these different exercises have in common in an
effort to exemplify the basic character of this new kind of
thinking.

Exercises to develop higher stages of knowledge on the
anthroposophical path of schooling draw on the three
faculties of Imagination, Inspiration and Intuition as a whole
organism if you like, a living configuration that cannot simply
be divided into separate parts. Despite this, the three aspects
of this organism can be clearly differentiated both in terms of
the demands they make on us and of the modes of experience
which they school. From 1905/06, we repeatedly find in
Rudolf Steiner's works exercises specifically oriented to each
of these three modes of perception.[3]

Inspiration as the middle of the three stages of higher
knowledge (transitions between which, though, must be
understood as fluid) is by its very nature the hardest to
grasp. It draws upon Imagination, on images gained at the
first stage which are still coloured by personal nuances, and
transforms them into 'objective Imagination' (see page 42).
At this stage of knowledge, in so far as we enter upon real
spiritual experience and encounter spirit beings, we are led
directly over into the state of Intuition. This transitional or

liminal quality is a fundamental characteristic of Inspiration.

The four soul habits or virtues we spoke of above, which Rudolf Steiner describes in his early schooling texts *Knowledge of the Higher Worlds* and *The Stages of Higher Knowledge*, are primarily oriented to the development of Inspiration. It is at the same time characteristic of this middle stage of cognition that in a sense we rediscover the whole path of schooling in the sequence and graded development of these four virtues. We can say that the exercise for the first virtue—which schools a capacity to distinguish truth from mere appearance—starts in the realm of imaginative knowledge, with the development of deepened and more autonomous thinking. The second and third exercises connect thinking with human heart forces in so far as we first practise proper estimation of truth and love for it, and then, through the 'complementary' or 'subsidiary' exercises, develop the twelve-petalled lotus in the heart region into a 'kind of organ of thinking' (page 23) These six 'subsidiary' exercises, arranged in specific order, together develop the third soul habit on the path towards Inspiration, by cleansing soul activities of arbitrary and subjective colouring. This is at the same time the preparation for the fourth stage, which is concerned with completely overcoming a 'personal way of viewing the world' and with liberation from the 'limits of our narrower self'. At the same time we here enter the spiritual realm, arriving at the stage of Intuition where the 'secrets of the world of spirit [...]' gain 'entry to our inner being' (page 13).[4]

The exercises for acquiring the faculty of Inspiration

transform the etheric body—as the bearer of habits and modes of thinking—so that the pupil can eventually learn to 'determine the condition of his etheric body himself'. As thinking is gradually liberated from sensory impressions during our passage through the four stages of soul habits, we successively establish focal points 'for the currents of the etheric body', which move down from the head through the larynx into the heart, or into its neighbourhood. Meditation and concentration exercises create these focal points, and 'the four habits bring them to maturity' (page 12).

By transforming the etheric body in this way, the pupil is gradually 'endowed with the "inner Word"'.[5] This means that the inner reality of things becomes available to him; he has developed 'steadfastness', 'inner strength' and 'moral courage' (page 63) and gained a power of orientation that enables him really to enter the world of spirit. This orienting capacity, evident in an immediate knowledge of what is true or false, in a power of resolve and presence of mind, is described by Rudolf Steiner as 'characteristic of heart thinking' (page 23).

As suggested above, transforming our feelings is the basis for developing heart thinking. This is because everything 'that underlies our feelings is really a cradle of surging Inspirations'.[6] Inner schooling is a matter of raising feeling into consciousness, transforming subjective, personal sentiments into ones that really correspond to the truth and reality of their object. On one occasion Steiner encapsulated this key concern of Inspiration by saying that 'the development of a sense and feeling for truth is the most essential thing for inspired knowledge'.[7]

This 'feeling for truth' can only develop, however, when the pupil gradually frees himself from the bonds of his own personality, his ordinary, self-concerned feelings. Education for inner freedom is thus at the same time about consolidating our moral strength. While schooling of morality must accompany all stages on the path of knowledge, alongside all meditation and concentration exercises, it is especially connected with the second mode of cognition, the development of Inspiration. Summarizing these stages in 1921, Rudolf Steiner said that knowledge becomes artistic through Imagination, moral through Inspiration and religious through Intuition (see page 101).

Chapter 1 of this volume collects early and fundamental comments by Steiner on the four virtues or soul habits. Besides the two published books *Knowledge of the Higher Worlds* and *The Stages of Higher Knowledge*, the chapter also contains notes of a private esoteric lesson in the summer of 1903 whose language and approach are still very reminiscent of the theosophical tradition.[8] In the lectures of 1910, the first two virtues are described with much detail and nuance, whereas the third and fourth seem here to be summarized, in a sense, in the suggestion that we should learn to live in contradictions, engaging with our whole soul in the most varied views and positions, as a key prerequisite for overcoming a 'personal mode of observing the world' (page 13). At a later date Steiner no longer presents the soul habits in the systematic four stages of his early writings. Nevertheless we can rediscover them in metamorphosis in other places in his works (see especially Chapter 7).

Passages in Chapter 2 concern the aspect of Inspiration in relation to the process of meditation. In his book *An Outline of Occult Science* (GA 13, 1910), Rudolf Steiner gives a detailed account of how the images created in meditation are extinguished or, as he says, how we can immerse ourselves in the 'image-forming soul activity' (page 33) as a key exercise for acquiring the faculty of Inspiration. From 1922 onwards he speaks in this context only of extinguishing meditatively created images, mostly in relation to aspects such as the experience of pre-existence or the acquiring of a spiritual vision of the cosmos, a new cosmology, which are connected with the stage of inspired knowledge.

Some exercises, relating specifically to the schooling of feelings, are gathered in Chapter 3. Here I decided not to cite excerpts from *Knowledge of the Higher Worlds* since the exercises for educating feeling life can be found in almost every chapter of that book, and are not easily sundered from their context. (The same applies to 'The Path of Knowledge' as given in Steiner's book *Theosophy* [1904, GA 9].) The chapter of the same name in *The Stages of Higher Knowledge* offers a good overview of this schooling of feelings at the stage of Inspiration.

In 1913, in several lectures, Steiner touched on an aspect of Inspiration that is presented in Chapter 4. He points out that Inspiration knowledge can be achieved through 'retaining the "Word" within the soul' (page 68), by consciously grasping, transforming or emancipating the power of language. In 1923 he took up this theme again in a somewhat altered form, and spoke of 'negative quiet' as an intensified, deeper state of silence. This, he says, enables us to 'hear spiritually what lives in the world of spirit' (pages 78 f.). Here the pupil receives the 'inner Word' which reveals the essence of things to him. Yet this state cannot be attained without experiencing the 'cosmic pain' (page 82) that always accompanies our entry into the world of spirit, and is inseparably part of the stage of Inspiration.

Chapter 5 compiles a few Inspiration exercises in relation to natural phenomena. It becomes clear that at the stage of Inspiration we are concerned with rendering sense perception inwardly transparent and thus penetrating through to the essence of things.

In Chapter 6 several texts were included that briefly summarize the nature of Inspiration and develop some aspects that have made their appearance in previous chapters. Passages from *Occult Science* are fundamental here. In comments he made in the lecture of 6 May 1922, Rudolf Steiner again gave a detailed account of an important aspect of heart thinking, of the 'knowledge that is more concentrated in the heart' (page 102). By developing Inspiration knowledge, the heart becomes a kind of sense organ for pre-birth experience, and thus for the spirit. In a public lecture on 16 November 1923 in The Hague, where he does not explicitly refer to the higher stages of knowledge as such, Steiner speaks of a key aspect of thinking with the heart when he accentuates the 'affinity of healthy perception' with 'human selflessness' (page 110).

In Chapter 7 there is a unique account by Steiner taken from his 1911 lectures *The World of the Senses and the World of the Spirit* (GA 134). There he names four soul states that must be achieved 'if thinking [...] is to enter into reality' (pages

117). These soul qualities which build upon each other and can thus be experienced as successive stages—wonder, reverence, wise harmony with world phenomena, surrender to the universe—are clearly reminiscent of the four soul habits (see Chapter 1). Though described here from a different aspect, we can discern a close similarity between the inner gesture and orientation of both these four-stage paths. In the first case, the fourth stage seeks an emancipation from the limits of the 'narrower self' whereas in the second the goal is 'surrender to the workings of the universe'. The two are the same, seen from different perspectives: from the standpoint of the pupil, firstly, and secondly from the view of the wider world. In these lectures Steiner wishes to show how human beings can rediscover the primordial ground of divine being from which have flowed both our moral ideals and the wisdom of nature—two things we must initially regard as contradictory. Heart thinking, Inspiration knowledge, develops through the fourfold path towards their common origin.

If we now examine what connects exercises that initially appear very diverse with the development of this Inspiration capacity, we can find that they have two basic gestures in common.

This is, firstly, the gesture of relinquishment, which can be discerned both in the extinguishing of previously created images in meditation (Chapter 3) and in a schooling of our feelings in so far as the pupil seeks to relinquish certain feelings rising from his personal sensibility (Chapter 3). The development of an 'inner silence in the soul' (page 75) also points in this direction (Chapter 4). Rudolf Steiner here describes this quietude not merely as a state of outer calm but as something that requires a further active step into 'negative silence'. He makes clear here what is involved in the practice of relinquishment in these exercises: ridding ourselves of, or restraining something with which we feel very deeply connected, whether images engendered in meditation, our naturally arising feelings or the expression of our own thoughts and ideas. Through such renunciation a certain kind of actively created vacuum or negative space arises, within which spiritual realities can reveal themselves. This gesture is especially apparent in Rudolf Steiner's suggestion that we can cancel a sensory perception so as to inwardly perceive, say, the quality of a colour or crystal (Chapter 5). By doing this we immerse ourselves in an experience of 'the life of our whole surroundings, otherwise perceived only as sense phenomena' (page 91).

But a second, complementary gesture also belongs here: the development of new, spirit-oriented feelings. These can arise, for instance, in relation to 'communications from a higher world' (page 60) when the pupil participates with his whole feeling soul in spiritual-scientific accounts of the nature of the human being or cosmic evolution. Or they are developed by expanding our 'human interest beyond merely natural concerns', so that we come to experience natural processes 'in the same way as we experience what occurs within our own being' (page 85). By means of all these exercises we develop not only a keen and immediate sense of truth but also connect ourselves with it existentially in such a way that we learn 'to feel pain in error and pleasure in truth' (page 24).

All exercises oriented to acquiring Inspiration are thus distinguished by this fundamental twofold quality: on the one hand a shedding of subjective, personal feeling elements that rise from within our natural being, and on the other a conscious engendering and cultivating of more objective feelings that arise from, and correspond to, reality.

And that is the gesture of heart thinking: by transforming our feeling, and gaining inner freedom through surrender of our own personality, we develop a thinking that corresponds to the spiritual reality of creatures and beings we seek to perceive, thus truly coming closer to 'all-embracing truth' (page 29).

1. Four Soul Habits to Develop Heart Thinking

Spiritual science describes *four* qualities which a person needs to acquire on the path of probation, as we can call it, in order to rise to higher knowledge. The *first* of these is the ability to distinguish in thoughts what is true from what is false, truth from mere opinion. The *second* quality is a proper appreciation of truth and reality as opposed to appearance. The *third* consists in [...] practising the six capacities: control of thoughts, control of actions, patience and tenacity, tolerance, faith, and equanimity. The *fourth* is love of inner freedom.

Nothing at all is gained by a merely rational understanding of what lies in these four qualities. They must be integrated into the soul to such a degree that they establish inner *habits* in us. Let us consider the first quality, for instance: the capacity to discern truth as opposed to appearance. We must school ourselves so that we quite naturally distinguish the essential from the inessential in whatever we encounter. And we can only school ourselves in this way if we keep repeatedly attempting to do so with patience and tranquillity whenever we observe something in the world around us. Ultimately our gaze will home in on the truth as naturally as it was once satisfied by the inessential. 'Everything transient is but a likeness:'[9] this truth becomes a self-evident conviction of the soul. And the same is true of our practice of the other four qualities.

Now the human being's subtle ether body does actually transform under the influence of these four soul habits. The first, the ability to 'distinguish truth from appearance', creates the centre in the head that we have spoken of, and prepares the centre in the larynx.[10] To *really* develop these, however, we need the concentration exercises referred to earlier. They form them, and the four habits bring them to maturity and fruition. Once the focal point in the region of the larynx has been prepared, a proper *appreciation* of the truth as opposed to inessential appearance brings about the free mastery of the etheric body and its enclosure in, and limiting by, the ramifying network we described above. If we succeed in this esteem for truth, we gradually begin to perceive spiritual realities. But we ought not to think that we need only undertake actions that appear important to a rational appraisal. The least action, each gesture, has something important about it in the great scheme of the universe, and it is a matter simply of being *aware* of this. We should properly estimate, not underestimate, the performance of daily actions.

We have already spoken of the six virtues that compose the third quality. These are connected with development of the twelve-petalled lotus in the heart region. As we have shown, the life-stream of the etheric body must be directed there. The fourth quality, the longing for inner liberation, serves to bring to maturity the ether organ in the heart region. If this quality becomes a habit of soul, we free ourselves from everything that involves *only* the capacities of our personal nature. We cease to consider everything only from our own particular point of view. The boundaries of our narrower self that bind us to this point of view now vanish, and the secrets of the world of spirit gain entry to our inner being. This is liberation, for what binds us in this way compels us to see people, things and creatures according to our personal predilections. The esoteric pupil must liberate himself from this personal mode of observing the world in order to become free and independent.

We can gather from this that spiritual-scientific teachings and precepts can exert a profound effect on our inmost nature. This applies to what has been said here about the four qualities. Precepts such as these can be found in one or another form in all world-views that recognize a realm of spirit. The founders of such world-views did not draw them from dull or obscure feelings, but gave them to humankind because they were great initiates. They formed their ethical precepts out of true knowledge. They knew that these rules and practices act upon our subtler or finer nature, and they sought to develop this subtler nature gradually in those who embraced their teachings. To live in accord with such a world-view means working to perfect ourselves spiritually. Only if we do this do we serve the world. Perfecting ourselves is nothing to do with narcissism: an imperfect person serves humanity and the world imperfectly. The better and more perfect we are, the better we serve the whole. A saying encapsulates this: 'The self-adorning rose adorns the garden.'[11] (GA 10 (1904–5), pp. 145–8.)

As soon as the soul withdraws its activity to some degree from the body, pernicious powers from the elemental realms can seize hold of it. A danger arises here in higher development.

We must therefore ensure that as soon as the soul withdraws from the body the latter is intrinsically available only for good elemental influences. If we fail to observe this an ordinary person will degenerate physically in a certain respect, and also morally, despite gaining entry to higher worlds. While the soul lives in higher regions, harmful powers infiltrate the dense physical body and the etheric body. This is why, when insufficient care is given, bad qualities that were kept down by the soul's balancing effect now come to the fore. People who previously displayed good, ethical qualities, can under such circumstances, when they approach higher worlds, give expression to all kinds of lower inclinations, self-obsession, untruthfulness, vindictiveness, anger and so on. But no one should let themselves be deterred by this fact from ascending into higher worlds. We just have to take care beforehand that such things will not occur. Our lower nature must be fortified and rendered impenetrable for dangerous elemental influences; and this can be done through conscious development of certain virtues. These virtues, described below, are cited in theosophical treatises dealing with spiritual development, and we have now seen why we must take care to cultivate them.

Firstly we must always seek to distinguish the eternal from the ephemeral in everything we encounter, and pay attention to the former. In every thing and creature we can intuit something that endures when the transient phenomenon fades and disappears. If I see a plant I can first observe it as it appears to my senses. That certainly should be done. And no one will discover the eternal and imperishable in things without first acquainting himself thoroughly with the ephemeral. Those who express anxiety that they will lose the 'freshness and naturalness of life' if they fix their gaze on imperishable spirit have not yet realized what is actually involved. Observing the plant I can come to see that there exists in it an enduring urge for life that will manifest in a new plant once this one has long faded and crumbled to dust. This way of observing the world is one we must absorb into our whole sensibility. And then we must bind our heart to all that is valuable and authentic, learning to value this more than transient and insignificant things. In all our feelings and actions we should keep our gaze fixed on the value something has for the whole. Thirdly we should develop in ourselves six qualities or virtues: control of our thoughts, control of actions, steadfastness, open-mindedness, trust in our surroundings and inner balance.

We achieve control of our world of thoughts if we seek to counteract the rapid and random flux of our thoughts and feelings that ordinarily surge in us continually. In daily life we are not in command of our thoughts. They impel us, and this is quite natural since life does drive us and we must surrender to its headlong rush. In ordinary life this will inevitably be so. But if we wish to rise to a higher world we must take brief moments, at least, in which we become master of our world of thoughts and feelings. Doing so, we place one thought at the centre of our reflections in complete inner freedom, in contrast to the way ideas otherwise usually impose themselves on us from without. Then we try to keep all thoughts and feelings that rise up in us at arm's length, and only to connect with the original thought whatever we choose to associate with it. Such an exercise has a beneficial effect on the soul and thus also on the body. It puts the latter into a harmonious condition so that it is protected from harmful influences when the soul is not acting directly upon it.

Control of actions similarly involves regulating them in inner freedom. A good way of beginning to do this is to decide to perform a regular action that one would not otherwise have done in the normal course of life. Usually our actions are elicited by what happens around and outside us. But the smallest action we take by our own intrinsic initiative takes us further in the direction indicated than anything which outward life demands or necessitates.

By steadfastness I mean the opposite of fluctuation between highs and lows, between ecstasy and gloom. We are driven back and forth between all kinds of moods. Pleasure makes us happy, pain depresses us. That is justified. But if we seek the path of higher knowledge we must know how to modify or moderate both pleasure and pain. We must learn 'steadfastness'. We must be able to surrender entirely to pleasure-inducing and painful experiences, but always walk through both these with dignity. Nothing should overwhelm us or disconcert us. This will not lead to lack of feeling but instead makes us firm and steadfast amidst life's surging waves, so that we always have mastery over ourselves.

An especially important quality is the 'sense for affirmation'. We can develop this by turning our attention to what is good, beautiful and useful in anything rather than accentuating what is blameworthy, ugly or contradictory. There is a beautiful Persian legend about Christ that typifies this virtue: a dead dog is lying on a road when Christ and his followers pass it by. All the others turn their gaze away from this ugly, stinking sight. Only Christ speaks admiringly of the animal's beautiful teeth. Likewise we can look for something commendable even in what is most abhorrent. If we seek it earnestly we will find it. What is fruitful in things is not what they lack but what they possess.

It is also important to develop the quality of 'open-mindedness'. We have all had our own experiences and gathered a certain sum of opinions in consequence. These become our guidelines in life. However self-evident it is to base our views on our experiences, it is important for someone who seeks spiritual development and higher knowledge to keep an open mind for anything new, anything as yet unknown to him. He will be very cautious about saying anything is impossible, or a ridiculous idea. Whatever his previous experiences have taught him he will be ready at any moment to learn something new that alters his opinion. We must relinquish any love of our own views.

Once the soul has acquired these five qualities a sixth arises by itself: inner balance, the harmony of spiritual powers. We must find in ourselves something like a spiritual emphasis that gives us stability and certainty in the face of everything drawing us in one direction or another. We must not avoid living fully and allowing everything to work upon us. The right thing is not to flee the fluctuating realities of life but the opposite: to give ourselves up entirely to life and still, nevertheless, to preserve inner equilibrium and harmony and the solid foundation it gives us.

Finally, the seeker can reflect on the 'will to freedom'. This is possessed by anyone who seeks the support and foundation for everything he does within himself. This is so hard to achieve because it requires a discreet balance between opening our minds to everything good and great while at the same time rejecting any and every kind of compulsion. It is so easy to say that external influences are incompatible with freedom; but what matters is that they should be reconciled within us. If someone tells me something and I accept it by the force and compulsion of his authority, then I am indeed unfree. But I am no less unfree if I close myself off from all good that I can receive and embrace in this way. Then the negative qualities I possess exercise a compulsion upon me within my own soul. Where freedom is concerned, it is not just a matter of resisting the compulsion of an external authority but above all also that of my own prejudices, opinions, emotions and feelings. Rather than submitting blindly to what we receive from without we can allow it to stimulate us, open ourselves to it without prejudice and then, if we choose, 'freely' accept and acknowledge it. An authority outside me should affect me only in so far as I say to myself: I become free precisely by choosing to follow what is good in these suggestions, and thus making it my own. And any authority vested in esoteric science wishes to influence a person in no other way than this. Such an authority gives what it has to offer not in order to gain power over the recipient but only so that the latter will become richer and freer thereby. (GA 12 (1905–8), pp. 28–35.)

If someone wishes to rise to higher stages of development [...] he must become a pupil of the spirit,[12] and develop within him the qualities that pertain to this. He must gradually develop four chief qualities.

The first is the capacity to distinguish between the eternal and the ephemeral. That is, we learn to perceive in everything ephemeral, in everything we observe, the shaping power in it that endures. In everything our senses perceive there dwells a power that tends towards crystallization just as salt [dissolved in] warm water forms crystals [as the water cools]. Soil is powdered mineral, and in the seed lives the power to become a plant and bear fruit. Likewise there is inherent in the vertebra the potential to develop into a cranium. The tiny lancelet, a marine creature consisting of little more than a nerve cord, gives us a microscopic reflection of the first living form in which the Logos manifested. The huge first fish, which consisted only of a gelatine-like mass, is the ancient ancestor whose vertebrae bore within them the potential to develop into fish, amphibians, mammals and the human being. And so we can see the physical human being simply as a transitory phenomenon that changes its mineral substances each day and whose senses will not remain as they now are, but will adapt to higher stages of human evolution, already bearing within them the capacity to transform.

The second quality that must be developed is an appreciation or valuing of what endures. Knowledge or insight becomes felt. We learn to rate the eternal higher than the ephemeral, whose value increasingly fades in our estimation. And thus, by developing these two first qualities, the spiritual pupil is led quite naturally to the third—to the development of certain inner capacities.

a) *Examining our thoughts.* The spiritual pupil must not allow himself to look at things from only one angle. We formulate a thought and hold it to be true but in fact it is only true in one aspect or from one perspective. Later we must view it again from the opposite angle, always considering the other side of the coin as well. Only by doing so do we learn to examine, and balance, one thought in terms of another.

b) *Examining our actions.* We live and act in the material world, and are placed into the realm of time. Given the wealth of phenomena in the world, we can only grasp hold of a small portion of them, and our actions are tied to particular, ephemeral circumstances. Daily meditation enables the spiritual pupil to collect himself and examine and control his actions. He will look only for what endures in them, and place value only on actions through which he can help and serve the higher development of his fellow human beings. He will relate the wealth of the world of phenomena to the highest, overarching unity.

c) *Tolerance.* The spiritual pupil will not allow feelings of attraction and repulsion to master him. He will seek to understand everyone, including criminals and saints, and although he experiences things emotionally he will form intellectual judgements. What is rightly acknowledged as bad or wrong from one perspective can from another be judged as necessary and consistent.

d) *Steadfastness.* Accepting happiness or unhappiness with equanimity; not letting these determine and influence us; not allowing joy and pain to lead us astray; keeping ourselves free from all external influences and pursuing our own direction.

e) *Faith.* The spiritual pupil should have a heart that is free, open and unprejudiced towards a higher spiritual realm. Even when he does not immediately recognize a higher truth, he should keep faith until he can come to own it through insight. If he were to adhere too strictly to the principle of 'testing everything and retaining the best', he would make his own judgement the measure of everything, placing himself above a higher spiritual realm, and closing himself off from its influx.

f) *Balance*. The last soul capacity would arise naturally as the outcome of all others, as balance, assurance and inner equilibrium. The spiritual pupil himself sets his direction of travel.

And then we can develop the fourth quality, the will for freedom, for the ideal. As long as we still live in the physical realm, we cannot attain full freedom, but we can nevertheless develop the will for freedom in ourselves, strive towards the ideal. We can emancipate ourselves from outer circumstances and no longer react to the impact or offence exerted on us from without. Instead we can make our own enduring inner law into the guideline of our thoughts and actions, living not in our ephemeral personality but in our individuality which endures and strives for oneness. (Private lesson, Berlin-Schlachtensee, summer 1903, GA 88, pp. 176–9.)

Imaginative cognition [. . .] when we really attain it, enables us to see into the world of spirit in a certain way.

This happens as follows. We have to spend a relatively long time inwardly immersing ourselves in resonant symbols or images that are drawn directly from life, or also certain phrases and formulations that encapsulate great world mysteries. Eventually we will notice—to begin with at the moment we wake up in the morning, and then also during the day when we divert our attention away from outward experiences—that something appears before us in the same way, basically, as the images and symbols we created, but now this stands before the soul like outer objects in ordinary awareness such as stones and flowers: things we know that we have not ourselves created. Over time, as we undergo preparation, and through the care with which we ourselves engender images and symbols, we become able to distinguish illusory images from true ones. If we really prepare ourselves thoroughly, learning to extinguish our own personal opinions, wishes, desires and sufferings from our higher existence, learning to see that something is not true just because we wish it to be so, and practising how to extinguish our own opinion, we will immediately be able to distinguish whether the image we see before us in this way is true or false.

Now—and this is important for this capacity to discriminate between true and false pictures—something will occur for someone who undergoes this inner development which we can only describe as thinking with the heart. This certainly arises in the course of our development as I described it yesterday. In ordinary life we have a sense of thinking with our head. Naturally this is only metaphorical; in fact we think with the spiritual organs that underlie the brain. But everyone understands what is meant by 'thinking with the head'. We have a quite different feeling about the kind of thinking that begins when we have made some progress on the path of inner development as described. We really have the feeling that what is otherwise localized in the head has shifted to the heart. However, it is not the physical heart that thinks, but the spiritual organ that develops in the region close to the heart, which we call the twelve-petalled lotus. This becomes a kind of organ of thinking; and the thinking which arises here is very different from ordinary thinking. As we all know, when we employ thinking ordinarily, we must consider and reflect in order to arrive at the truth: we must pass from one idea to the next, from one point to other logically connected points. And by embarking on logical reflections we eventually arrive at what we call truth, knowledge—a kind of knowledge achieved through ordinary thinking. It is a different matter when we seek to know truth through real symbols, as described. These true symbols appear before us like outward objects, but thinking about them cannot be confused with ordinary head thinking. You see, whether something is true or false, whether we have this or that to say about a thing or a reality of the higher worlds, does not require reflections as in ordinary thinking, but arises directly and immediately. The moment the pictures stand before us, we know what is to be said about them to ourselves or others. It is this immediacy of knowledge that characterizes heart thinking. (Lecture in Vienna, 29 March 1910, GA 119, pp. 217–19.)

If you wish to embark on higher development, you will need to spend some time on schooling your logical thinking. But you will also have to cast all this aside again in order to arrive at thinking with the heart. What remains from your schooling in logic will be the habit of conscientiousness in relation to discovering and holding to the truth in higher worlds. If you undergo this schooling you will not regard any and every illusory or arbitrary image as a true imagination, or interpret it in a random way. Instead you will have the inner strength to approach reality, seeing and interpreting it in the right light. This is precisely why it is so necessary to undergo good, subtle preparation: because then we must return to our immediate feeling and apprehension, have the sense of whether something is true or false. To put it exactly, the following must happen. Whereas we deliberate in our ordinary thinking, in relation to higher things we must have schooled our soul so that it can immediately distinguish whether these things are true or false.

Another good preparation for such immediate apprehension is to acquire a capacity, to some degree, that is present only to a very limited extent in ordinary life. Normally, most people would feel pain, might even cry out, if one were to stick a needle in them or pour hot water over their head or suchlike. But how many people feel something resembling pain if another person makes a foolish or absurd statement? Many people find this perfectly bearable. If you wish to develop the immediate apprehension I have described, the direct experience of something in the world of Imagination being true or false, you will need to train in yourself a sense that error really hurts you, really causes pain, and that the truth you perceive brings you pleasure and joy also already here in physical life. Yet learning this is a tiresome and tiring business, apart from all other difficulties. The preparation for entering higher worlds can be gruelling. To pass error or truth by with indifference is much easier for us, less stressful, than feeling pain in error and pleasure in truth. There is no lack of opportunity today to experience pain at the foolish things we read in books or newspapers. To feel suffering and pain in relation to untruth, ugliness or wickedness, even if it is not directed at us, and to feel pleasure in all that is beautiful, true and good, even if it does not directly concern us, belongs to the schooling we must undergo if we wish to learn heart thinking, and rise to a level where, as has been described, we have an immediate feeling in response to an image that appears before us.

There is another thing, too, that belongs to our preparation for rising into the world of Imagination. In feeling in pictures what is intrinsic to a higher world, we have to acquire something else that we do not ordinarily have: we must learn to think in a new way about what usually strikes us as either contradictory or concordant. In daily life two assertions about the same circumstances can often appear contradictory. Imagine that two people go to the same region but experience it quite differently from each other. The two may describe the same things in very different ways, and yet they may both be right from their own perspective. Let us assume that one of them tells us he has been in a healthy place, with plenty of fresh air, and that this gave him back his health; and then another, who has been to the same place, says that actually it's a very unhealthy region, and that he grew sick and weak there. Both of them may be right. The first might have a strong constitution. Perhaps he was overworked and tired when he got to this place he's describing, and found the air very refreshing and enlivening, while the other, say, was sickly, someone who found the climate and all that fresh air hard to cope with. What re-enlivens one person and gives him back his health can prove very negative for another, and have a debilitating effect. This is because they were different people and arrived there with different constitutions. If we take everything into account, contradictory assertions can in fact often be reconciled in ordinary life.

But things become much more complex when we rise into higher worlds. Let us imagine that someone has heard some comment in a lecture, and in another lecture he hears something else that appears to contradict it. He now applies the standard usually applied in life, and assumes that one of these statements cannot be true since it contradicts the other. We can take something close to home as an example. In one of my past lecture series, someone heard me say that as a person descends to a new birth we can observe him hurrying, as it were, through astral space at great speed, to seek the place where he wishes to incarnate. I once made this observation, which is certainly correct, in a lecture series I was giving. In this current series, on the other hand, I have said that the human spirit works for a long, long time on the inherited characteristics it will eventually receive at birth— that it collaborates on the qualities it eventually finds in the family and people into which it is born. Applying ordinary standards of judgement, we can of course easily find this a little contradictory. Yet both are real experiences. It is not always possible to convey everything at once: when we describe one experience we cannot always, of course, describe the other, corresponding experience at the same time. Both are true. A metaphor might help resolve the contradiction. Have you ever had the experience that someone makes something very carefully for five or six days, but on the seventh day he can't find it? He has to search everywhere in his room to find where he put it. For five or six days, he has prepared the whole thing, and on the seventh it's gone and he has to look for it everywhere. Something similar can happen in the higher worlds. We prepare our incarnation, but since the experiences connected with this are very complex it is possible that at the moment the person is actually descending from higher worlds and wishes to unite with the physical and etheric body, he has to search for them because his consciousness is obscured in a certain way. And because this darkening of consciousness occurs, the person has to search with a lower degree of consciousness for what he prepared at a higher level of awareness.

This example can show us that something particular can be necessary when we rise into these higher worlds: we must always be aware of the fact that in the world of imaginations one or another thing will present itself as a certain picture. If we have acquired a strong enough feeling enabling us, through the heart's thinking, to accept the truth of the picture, then it can happen on another occasion, when we are pursuing a different path, that we arrive at another imagination that appears quite different. And once again our immediate feeling tells us that it is true. Naturally this can be initially confusing for someone who enters the higher world, the world of Imagination. But this confusion is resolved by recognizing it at the appropriate moment.

We can gain the right stance, the right relationship to these circumstances if we seek our own I in the world of imaginations. We have described how, standing outside our I, we look back upon it.[13] As we pass by the Guardian of the Threshold, we have this objectively before us. But we can seek this I once, twice, three times, and each time we will see different pictures. If we approach this fact with the conditioning acquired in the physical world, we could easily become extremely confused and say: I recognized how I am in higher worlds, but the second time I found myself again, and was quite different, and on the third occasion different again. That is certainly the case. The moment we enter the imaginative world, by means of the schooling described, and see an image of our I, we must be clear that we can discern twelve different pictures of it. There are twelve different pictures of each I. And we can only fully understand our own I when we have looked back upon it from without from twelve different points of view. This view of the I from without is exactly like something that appears in the relationship of the twelve zodiac pictures to the sun. Just as the sun passes through the twelve constellations and has a different power in each, just as it appears in spring in a certain constellation, then moves on and, during the course of the year, passes through all twelve constellations and thus shines down on the earth from twelve different perspectives, so the human I also shines upon itself from twelve different angles, illumines itself from twelve different angles when it looks back from the higher world.

And this is why, when we rise into higher worlds, we must not make do with a single perspective. We must train ourselves in this capacity to avoid confusion. We can only do so when we have accustomed ourselves in the physical world to recognize that seeing something from a single point of view is not the be-all and end-all in life. (Lecture in Vienna, 29 March 1910, GA 119, pp. 223–8.)

This is a skill we must develop: being able to leave ourselves behind, and look at things as it were with someone else's eyes, from a different point of view. Only this can lead to all-embracing truth. Instead of looking at only one side of a rose bush we can move around it and find different views, take up different positions or photograph it from different angles. By this means we school ourselves in a capacity we really must possess as soon as we enter higher worlds, and we can learn this already in the physical world. To enter higher worlds with a personal standpoint will sow confusion in us—we will see not truth but illusion, because we are bringing our own personal opinion into this world.

And to develop heart thinking we must have the strength to leave ourselves behind, really to become quite foreign to ourselves, and look back on ourselves from without. In our ordinary consciousness, we stand at a certain place and when we say, 'This is me,' we mean the sum of our beliefs and what we stand for. But when we enter the higher worlds, we must be able to leave our ordinary personality behind in its place, emerge from ourselves, look back on ourselves, and say with the same feeling: 'That is you.' Our previous I must really become a 'you' to us in the right way. Just as we say 'you' to someone else, so we must be able to say 'you' to ourselves. This shouldn't be theoretical but a real experience. We have already seen that this capacity can be acquired through inner schooling. It is not so very difficult—it requires us to do relatively simple things; and then we acquire the right to think with the heart. True accounts of the higher worlds proceed from this heart thinking. Even if, outwardly, they may often appear to be logical reflections, there is nothing in accounts that are really brought down from higher worlds that has not been thought with the heart. What is described in this way from the perspective of spiritual science has been experienced with the heart. But someone who must seek to describe what he experiences with the heart has to pour it into thought forms that are comprehensible to others.

This is the difference between real spiritual science and subjectively experienced mysticism. Subjective mysticism is available to all: it remains confined within your personality; it cannot be communicated to someone else, and does not really concern anyone else either. But true, genuine mysticism arises from the capacity to have imaginations, to receive impressions from the higher worlds and to classify and order these impressions with the thinking of the heart, just as we rationally order and classify physical things.

And this in turn is related to the fact that something like heart's blood is connected with the truths given from higher worlds—that they are coloured by heart thinking. They may appear abstract, and have been moulded into forms of thought, but they are infused with the heart's blood because they were directly experienced in the soul. The moment we have developed heart thinking, we know as we enter the imaginative world that what we see before us, which appears as a vision, is in fact the expression of a spirit and soul reality that stands behind it, just as the red colour of the rose here is the outward expression of the material rose. The seer directs his spiritual gaze to the imaginative world, receives the impression of blue or violet, or hears a tone, or has a sense of warmth or cold. And he knows through the thinking of his heart that this is not mere fantasy, not mere hallucination, but the expression of a being of spirit and soul, just as the red is the expression of the material rose.

And thus we live our way into realities: we have to leave ourselves behind and connect with these beings and realities themselves. That is why all enquiries into the world of spirit are at the same time connected with surrender of our own personality to a much greater degree than occurs with outward experiences and impressions. We are drawn more intensively into things, we dwell within things themselves. Dwelling within them we experience at first hand their good and bad qualities, their beauty and ugliness, their truth and falsehood. Where others immediately perceive a fault or error in the physical world, the spiritual scientist must not only observe an error or fault in the imaginative world but also live through it in pain. Whether we like it or not, we must not only witness something that is ugly or detestable but inwardly experience it. The schooling described, which is especially fitting for people today, enables us to fully experience the good, true and beautiful in a phenomenon, but also the bad and ugly, the error, without being caught and captured by it, and without losing ourselves. You see, the heart's thinking, acquired through the right preparation, leads to our ability to practise discernment through and within the immediacy of feeling. (Lecture in Vienna, 29 March 1910, GA 119, pp. 231–3.)

2. Extinguishing Images

We can acquire knowledge through Inspiration and Intuition only by practising soul-spiritual exercises. They are similar to those that have been described to achieve Imagination through 'inner contemplation' (meditation).[14] But whereas the exercises leading to Imagination draw on images from the physical world of the senses, those leading to Inspiration increasingly depart from this connection with physical things. To clarify what is needed here let us think [. . .] of the image of the Rose Cross. As we contemplate this inwardly we have before us an image whose parts are drawn from the world of the senses: the black colour of the cross, the red roses and so forth. However these elements are put together to form the Rose Cross in a way that is not founded in the physical world. If the spiritual pupil now tries to make the black cross and the red roses vanish entirely from his mind as things of sensory reality, retaining in his soul only the spiritual activity which composed them into a whole, then he has the means to practise a form of meditation which will gradually lead him to Inspiration. One can ask oneself roughly the following question: What did I do inwardly to compose the cross and roses into an image? I will seek to hold fast to what I did (my own soul process); the image itself, though, I will erase from my mind. Then I will try to feel within me everything my soul did to create the image. But I will not picture this image itself. Instead I will live very inwardly in my own activity, which created the image. Rather than contemplating an image, therefore, I will contemplate my own image-forming soul activity. One has to do this in relation to many images, and this will lead to knowledge through Inspiration. Here is another example. Contemplate the thought of a growing and then fading plant. First let the image of a gradually developing plant grow from a seedling, putting forth one leaf after another and then eventually forming a flower, followed by fruit. Then follow it further in your mind as it begins to fade and die, until it has vanished completely again. Through this contemplation we gradually arrive at a feeling of growth and decay which the image of the plant merely embodies. From this feeling, as we continue to persevere with the contemplation, an imagination can form of the metamorphosis which underlies such physical growth and decay. But if we seek the corresponding inspiration, we must do the exercise differently. We must instead reflect on our own activity of soul which has acquired from the image of the plant the thought of growth and decay. We must let the plant itself fade entirely from our mind and now only contemplate what we ourselves did inwardly. We can only rise to Inspiration by undertaking this kind of exercise. Initially the spiritual pupil will find it hard to understand all that is involved in embarking on such an exercise. This is because, accustomed as we are to allowing outward impressions to determine our inner life, we immediately feel uncertain: we enter a completely fluctuating realm as we try to unfold a life of soul that has shed all connection with outward impressions. To a still greater degree than we need when forming imaginations, the spiritual pupil must realize, in relation to these Inspiration exercises, that he should only embark on

them if, at the same time, he accompanies them with
measures that can safeguard and consolidate his capacity for
judgement, his life of feeling and his whole character. If he
take such precautions, he will gain in two ways. Firstly, the
exercises will not unbalance his personality when he practises
supersensible perception; and secondly, he will at the same
time acquire the ability to really perform what these exercises
require. We can only say that these exercises are difficult as
long as we have not yet acquired a very particular frame of
mind and soul, certain feelings and perceptions. But we can
soon understand these exercises, and also gain the ability to
do them, if with patience and perseverance we cultivate in
ourselves inner qualities that help supersensible perceptions
to bud and grow in us. We will gain a great deal if we
accustom ourselves to looking inwards, but in a way less
concerned with brooding on ourselves than with ordering
and assimilating what we have experienced in life. We will
find that we enrich our thoughts and feelings when we relate
one life experience to another. We will see to what degree we
can then not only gain new experiences and new impressions
but also inwardly assimilate old ones. If we can set to work by
allowing our experiences, and even the opinions we have
formed, to play against each other as if we ourselves were not
involved at all in our own sympathies and antipathies, in our
personal interests and feelings, we will be preparing a very
good soil for supersensible powers of perception to germi-
nate. In fact we will be developing what can be called a *rich
inner life*. Most important of all, however, is to create a balance and equilibrium of soul qualities. It is all too easy for us
to succumb to one-sidedness when we give ourselves up to

certain soul activities. But when we realize the benefit of inner reflection and of dwelling in our own thought world, we can develop such an inclination for this that we start to close ourselves off increasingly from outer impressions. Yet this leads to inner desiccation and aridity. We get furthest, by contrast, if at the same time as developing the ability to withdraw inwardly we also preserve a receptivity to all outer impressions. And this does not need to mean just supposedly 'important' impressions. *All* of us, in *any* circumstances—however impoverished and straitened—can experience enough if we just stay open and receptive. We don't even need to go searching for impressions; they are everywhere to be found. Of special importance also is *how* we assimilate our experiences. For instance, we may discover that someone we or others look up to has a characteristic that we must regard as a flaw. This observation can lead us in one of two directions. We can simply say that we can no longer look up to this person as we did before. Or we can ask ourselves how this person we look up to can have that particular flaw. Can I look at this flaw and discover how it may have come about not just as a flaw but as something inherent in this person's life, and perhaps even as a direct result of his fine attributes? If we ask ourselves this we may find that there is no need at all for the flaw to diminish our respect. This outcome will invariably teach us something, will have added something to our understanding of life. But a word of caution. The good gained by such an outlook might mislead us to excuse all kinds of things, or even become accustomed to overlooking anything deserving of censure. The benefit of positive thinking for our inner development might lead us to overlook flaws we should recognize. In fact, understanding rather than merely blaming someone for their flaws will not benefit our development. What we need to practise is, irrespective of any gain or loss to ourselves, to respond on its own terms to any such conduct in each separate instance. It is certainly true that we cannot learn by judging a person's flaw but only by understanding it. But if, for the sake of understanding, we throw the baby out with the bathwater and relinquish all displeasure, we will not get very far either. Once again this is to do with avoiding one-sidedness, with cultivating balance and good measure in our soul faculties.

This is especially true of a quality of soul that is of outstanding importance for our development, which we can call a feeling of *devotion*. If we can develop this feeling within us, or if we possess it as a natural gift, we find good soil for supersensible powers of perception to flourish. If we were able in our childhood and youth to look up admiringly to people as to high ideals, then in the depths of our soul will live something within which supersensible perceptions can thrive. And likewise someone who in later life, with mature judgement, can look up to the starry heavens and wonderingly feel there the revelation of higher powers will also make himself ripe for perceiving supersensible worlds. The same is true of someone who can marvel at the powers that hold sway in human life. And it is of no little importance if, as a mature adult, we can feel awe or reverence for others whose worth we intuit or think we perceive. Only where such devotion exists can a window open into higher worlds. Those who cannot feel it will not make much headway on the path of knowledge. Someone who does not wish to acknowledge anything in the world will not penetrate the true nature of things. Yet if we allow feelings of devotion and reverence to entirely kill off our *healthy* self-awareness and self-confidence, we likewise sin against the law of balance and equilibrium. The spiritual pupil will work continually on himself to become ever more mature; but in this case he is right to have trust in himself and his own being, and to believe that his powers will grow and develop. If we develop the right feelings in this direction, we come to see that powers lie concealed within us which we can draw forth. Therefore, where I see that I should respect and revere a quality because it is greater than my own, I do not need only to revere but I can also be sure that I will be able to develop in myself everything that will bring me to the level at which this revered person stands.

The greater our capacity to attend to certain occurrences in life that do not immediately accord with views we already hold, the easier it is for us to create foundations upon which we can raise ourselves towards higher worlds. Let me illustrate this with an example. Someone finds himself in a situation where he can either do something or not do it. His judgement tells him to do it. Yet an inexplicable something remains in his sensibility and prevents him from acting. Now it is possible to ignore this inexplicable something, and simply accomplish the action in line with our judgement. But we might heed this inexplicable something and not act. If we delve a little deeper it can become apparent that taking the action in question would have led to disaster, and that not to have done it was a blessing. An experience such as this can take our thinking in a very particular direction. We can come to see that there lives in us something that guides us better than the degree of discrimination we currently possess. I have to keep an open mind for this 'something in me' which my power of judgement is not yet mature enough to encompass. It has a very beneficial effect on the soul if we can attend to such instances in life. It becomes apparent to us that there is more within us than we can rationally evaluate. Such attentiveness helps enlarge our soul life. But here too there is a danger of unbalance. Anyone who sought to habitually disregard his judgement because 'intuitions' prompt him to do certain things could become the plaything of all kinds of inchoate drives. Such a habit could quickly lead to lack of judgement and superstition, and any kind of superstition is dire for the spiritual pupil.

We only acquire the ability to enter spiritual realms in an authentic way by carefully guarding ourselves against superstition, fantasy and reverie. We do not rightly enter the world of spirit if we are delighted to experience something that 'human thinking cannot grasp'. A penchant for the 'inexplicable' makes no one a spiritual pupil. The latter must completely shed the prejudice that a mystic is someone who assumes there are 'unexplained and unfathomable' things wherever this is easy and convenient. A spiritual pupil has the proper sense of things if he recognizes that hidden powers and beings are everywhere, but also that what has not yet been discovered and understood can be if we develop the powers to do so.

There is a certain frame of mind important to a spiritual pupil at every stage of his development. We should avoid a one-sided focus on discovering answers to questions, instead always seeking to know how we can develop this or that capacity in ourselves. When I have developed a particular capacity in me through inner, patient endeavour, then answers to certain questions will also become apparent. Spiritual pupils will always cultivate this outlook, and it will lead them to ever greater maturity, and to a willingness to refrain from insisting on answers to certain questions. They will wait until these answers are granted them. But here too we might become one-sided, and would then make little headway. The spiritual pupil can harbour a sense that he will eventually be able to answer even the loftiest questions, commensurate with his developing powers. So here again, balance and equilibrium play a very important role in our outlook. (GA 13 (1910), pp. 359–68.)

Practice of the inspiration exercise will add a new capacity to those previously developed: that of ridding our mind of the images on which we have been dwelling in meditation. Here it must be expressly stated that the ability required is that of ridding the mind of images previously voluntarily created in meditation, and to do this, likewise, freely and voluntarily. Ridding ourselves of images that have not voluntarily been created in our mind will not suffice. We need greater inner energy to erase images we first developed in meditation than to erase thoughts that entered our mind in other ways. We need this greater energy to make headway in supersensible cognition.

In this way we can succeed in achieving a wakeful but entirely empty state of soul. We rest in wakeful consciousness. If we experience this state in full and calm awareness, the soul will fill with spiritual realities just as the senses fill with physical sense impressions. This is the state of Inspiration. We experience our inner life within the cosmos as we otherwise feel our inner life to be within the physical organism. But we know that we are now experiencing the life of the cosmos in us, that the spiritual realities and occurrences in the cosmos reveal themselves as our own inner soul life. At the same time we must always retain the ability to freely return from this inner experience of the cosmos to our ordinary state of awareness. Then we can also always relate what we experience in Inspiration to the experience of our ordinary consciousness. In the cosmos perceived with our senses we can find a reflection of what we experienced spiritually. The process resembles one in which we compare a new experience with an old memory that surfaces in our mind. The spiritual perception we have is like a new experience, and our sense perception of the cosmos is like the memory picture.

The spiritual vision of the cosmos we gain in this way is different from that arising in Imagination. In the latter arise general pictures of etheric occurrences, whereas in Inspiration pictures of spiritual beings appear that hold sway within these etheric phenomena. What we know in the physical sense world as sun, moon, planets and the fixed stars are now rediscovered as cosmic beings. And our own soul-spiritual experience appears enclosed within the sphere in which this cosmic world of beings holds sway. Only now does the human physical organism become comprehensible, for its form and life are embodied not only in what the human senses can perceive but in beings that hold creative sway in the sense world's realities. Everything experienced in this way through Inspiration remains entirely hidden to ordinary consciousness. We would only become aware of it if we experience our breathing process as we do our processes of sense perception. For ordinary consciousness, the cosmic activity between the human being and the world remains hidden. Yoga philosophy seeks to access a cosmology by transforming the breathing process into a process of sense perception. This is not something that we in the West should imitate in modern times. During the course of humanity's evolution we have acquired an organism that renders *such* yoga exercises invalid. By practising them we would never entirely separate from our organism and therefore would fail in the need to leave our physical and etheric organism untouched. Such exercises were fitting for a past era of human evolution. But what they achieved must now be achieved as I described above in relation to Inspiration knowledge. By this means we experience in full consciousness what humanity in past eras experienced in the form of waking dreams. (September 1922, GA 25, pp. 27–9.)

The faculty of Imagination first gives us pictures of supersensible reality while Inspiration points us further into this reality. We create the possibility of Imagination through meditation, concentration, and we achieve Inspiration by developing, through an inner technique, another capacity that in ordinary life is quite rightly not especially valued. This involves observing in such a way that we become clear what it means to forget, to discard a thought picture from our mind. We have to practise a meditative, self-induced forgetting, an eliminating of thoughts, and thereby school ourselves in the ability to discard and finally extinguish imaginative life, the life in images that we have previously worked to acquire. If we have only succeeded in having imaginations, we cannot yet penetrate spiritual reality. This is only possible by eradicating these imaginations that first arise, if you like, as a realization of the imaginative capacity. They are something, you see, more or less self-created. We have to clear and empty our mind, voluntarily employing the act of forgetting on this imaginative life. And thus we learn to see what is meant by living in a powerful state of wakeful awareness that does not have thought pictures but, by first creating imaginations has developed inner energy, and has now relinquished its content. This is what we have to learn, and then we rise from Imagination to knowledge gained through Inspiration, and discover that we are touched by a spiritual reality that reveals itself to us in a soul-spiritual process that can be compared with the rhythmic process of breathing. The latter involves us drawing outer air into ourselves, inwardly permeating it and then expelling it in a different form after having, in a sense, united with it. In the same way we come to know a process of spirit and soul that depends on us experiencing the inner power of consciousness that we have gained, being able to soul-spiritually inhale into ourselves this awareness strengthened through Imagination. And by this means, objective Imagination lights up within this strengthened awareness. We breathe in the world of spirit, it enters us, we become one with it, living beyond ourselves: a rhythmic interplay with the world of spirit begins.

In ancient India people employed instinctive ways of seeking higher knowledge. As you may know, these instinctive efforts, embodied in yoga, employ the breathing process in a physical way so as to experience this breathing itself as a process of spirit and soul. In oriental yoga practice, breathing—inhaling, holding the breath and exhaling—is regulated in a particular way, with devotion and surrender to this breathing process. In a sense the spirit and soul are here sucked out of the breathing process. The breathing process is sundered from the mind by pushing it in and down, and then the spirit and soul remain over. This process that people underwent in yoga practice is something we can no longer do today, given our modern organism, and we ought not to do it. It would cast us down into the physical organism. Our life of soul no longer occupies the domain that it did in ancient India. There it tended more towards sensibility whereas ours tends more towards intellectualism. And in the sphere of intellectualism, yoga breathing would risk destroying our physical organization. When living in an intellectual realm we have to use exercises such as those described in my book *Knowledge of the Higher Worlds*, which remain purely in the domain of soul and spirit. At the most—and this only rarely or not at all in most cases—they allow a hint of the corporeal breathing process to enter. But our exercises oriented to attaining Imagination in the purely soul-spiritual realm essentially unfold in the sphere we experience when we do geometry and mathematics. What must be done to achieve Inspiration likewise unfolds in this sphere.

Through Inspiration it becomes possible to acquire awareness of an external world of spirit and soul, a soul-spiritual objectivity. (Lecture in Stuttgart, 3 September 1921, GA 78, pp. 120–3.)

But then we can try to go further in supersensible knowledge, further developing our meditative practice. In meditation we first dwell on certain thoughts or contexts of thought, and this strengthens our inner life. But this is not yet sufficient for entering fully into the supersensible world. To do this we also have to practise not just dwelling on thought pictures, not just concentrating our whole soul on these thoughts, but also being able to discard them again from our mind voluntarily. Just as we can look at something then look away again in the physical world, so we must learn as we develop supersensible capacities to first focus intently on an inner content and then be able to eliminate it from the soul again.

In ordinary life this may not always be easy. Consider how difficult many people find it to dismiss thoughts from their mind. Sometimes an unpleasant thought can pursue some-one for days on end, and seems impossible to be rid of. But it becomes much more difficult once we have accustomed ourselves to focusing on a thought. A thought content on which we have meditatively concentrated eventually begins to hold us fast, and we must make strenuous efforts to get rid of it again. For instance, when we have practised long enough, then we can succeed in removing from our mind again this whole retrospective review of our life back to birth which I spoke of—this whole ether body, as I call it, this time body.

This is a stage of development, of course, which we have to endeavour to achieve. We must first grow ready for it; by extinguishing meditative thoughts we must acquire the strength to eliminate this inner colossus, this soul giant in us. The whole terrible 'shark'* of our life hitherto, from this present moment back to birth, stands before us: we have to get rid of it. If we do, something will occur that I would call 'more wakeful consciousness'. Then we are simply awake and alert without any content in our wakeful mind. But now this begins to fill. Just as air streams into the lungs that need it, so now the real spiritual world streams into our empty consciousness, which has arisen in the way I have described.

That is Inspiration. Something streams in that is not some kind of finer substance, but which relates to substance as positive relates to negative. The opposite of substance now streams into the being of ours that has been freed of the ether. That is the important thing: to realize that spirit is not just a finer, more etheric substance. That isn't so. If we call substance 'positive' we must call spirit 'negative' in relation to it. It is like having the great fortune of 5 shillings in your wallet. I spend one, then I have 4; another, then I have 3; and so on until I have nothing left. Then I can start accruing debts. When I owe a shilling, I have less than no shillings.

Having disposed of the etheric body by this means, I do not enter a still finer ether, but instead something that is opposite to the ether just as my debts are opposite to my assets. And only now do I learn the nature of spirit. The spirit enters us through Inspiration; and the first thing we now experience is what lived in a world of spirit, before we were conceived, with our soul and with our spirit: the pre-existent

---

* Steiner used specifically this word in German.

life of our soul and spirit. Previously we looked back in the ether to our birth. Now we look back beyond birth or conception to the world of spirit and soul, and can perceive ourselves as we were before we descended from spiritual worlds and acquired a physical body through heredity.

For initiation knowledge these things are not intellectually invented philosophical truths but experiences, though ones that must first be acquired through schooling and preparation as described. And so the first thing we learn when we enter the world of spirit is the truth of the pre-existence of the human soul or the human spirit; we learn to have direct vision of eternity. (Lecture in Oxford, 20 August 1922, GA 305, pp. 86–8.)

To enlarge our cosmology, meditative life must be extended too. We can do this as follows. The soul first accustoms itself to dwell with the whole scope of its faculties upon a thought or thought complex that it can encompass, to dwell on this and keep dwelling on it, thus entering into intensified activity that is at last sundered from the physical organism and unfolds in a purely etheric realm. That is only the first stage. Then the soul must succeed in eliminating from consciousness these very thoughts on which it has been dwelling. In the same intentional way as the soul allowed thoughts to be present in the mind and concentrated fully on them, it must now succeed in discarding them entirely and thus enter into a state of fully conscious wakefulness without any inner content acquired like sensory impressions or thoughts. The soul must be awake, but contain none of the contents usually filling the ordinary mind.

Thus when the soul creates a state of fully alert but empty consciousness, and employs inner strength to sustain this emptiness of the soul while fully conscious, it will eventually come to a point when a cosmic content of spirit and soul flows into the empty mind—a content hitherto unknown, a new world of spirit, a spiritual environment if you like. This is the stage of Inspiration, which succeeds the stage of supersensible cognition achieved in Imagination.

Once we have this ability to receive a soul-spiritual content into our emptied mind through Inspiration, then we also receive that organization which I [...] called the human astral organism: the astral organism that lived in a world of spirit and soul before we descended to the earth and clothed ourself in a physical and etheric body. We become acquainted with our own soul-spiritual life before we were conceived, before birth. We come to know the astral organization which at death again departs from the physical human being and lives on in the world of spirit and soul. Thus inspired cognition gives us knowledge of the astral organism that expresses itself in ordinary consciousness as thinking, feeling and will.

At the same time we come to know the spiritual cosmos. The physical cosmos presents itself to our senses and to the thinking bound up with it; but now we have the spiritual cosmos before us. And what unfolds from this spiritual cosmos as the human being's physical organization, and also his etheric organization, is much more real than the sense perceptions we otherwise receive in our ordinary mind. It is true to say that what flows into us through Inspiration and gives us a soul life independent of the body can be compared with our breathing, our inhaling of actual oxygen. Through inspired knowledge we also gain a more precise understanding of the human breathing process, and the rhythmic blood circulation process associated with it. We gain a real vision of the human rhythmic system, of all rhythmic processes within us, through Inspiration. We gain insight into how the astral organization works within our rhythmic system. And moreover we come to see how the astral organism, clothed in the physical and etheric organism, is connected with breathing, indeed with our whole rhythmic organism, and how it comes to infuse the rhythm of breathing and blood circulation.

But by this means we can also gain insight into what in us is only physical and etheric heredity, what is subject to the laws of heredity, earthly laws, as opposed to what we bring with us from the supersensible, extra-telluric world, from the cosmos: the being of soul and spirit that enters the earthly world and only dresses itself with, or clothes itself in, the physical and etheric organism. We can then distinguish between inherited characteristics and what we have brought with us from a world of spirit into physical existence. (Lecture in Dornach, 7 September 1922, GA 215, pp. 32–4.)

But if we wish to get beyond this first level of supersensible cognition, then we must develop a second stage of perception within the soul. After drawing on our thinking at the first stage of cognition, activating and strengthening this in order to grasp and encompass ourselves within our etheric body, at the second stage we must in turn discard from our mind everything that we gain in this way through strengthened thinking. Having first intensively created a conscious content in our soul by concentrating to the utmost, we must now let this go again. You know what occurs when we must eliminate the ordinary content of our soul, the world which our senses give us: we fall asleep. We succumb gradually to a torpidity of soul. This must not happen now, and does not happen. Yes, it is difficult to eliminate again a soul content that we have energetically created in our mind. It is harder to get rid of this content than the content of our ordinary mind. But when we succeed in doing this, something occurs that never otherwise does. An utter emptiness fills our mind. Through what we underwent as we intensively experienced our own etheric body, we become able to disregard, to abstract ourselves from, the sense world and from all ordinary thinking. We live then in a higher region. And if we in turn eliminate this higher region once more, our own life tableau, our mind, becomes empty and we enter a condition that is significant for higher cognition: that of mere wakefulness, devoid of any soul content. We direct our strengthened, empowered mind out into the emptiness of the world. We do not fall asleep as we do this, but remain awake, and for a moment we face nothing but the void. This does not last long. If we have kept nothing but alert wakefulness in our consciousness, really empty consciousness, then a world of spirit enters us which is not our etheric body, not what has an affinity with it, but rather a world of spirit that is initially at a very far remove. Into our empty, waking consciousness the real world of spirit penetrates. But this emptied mind and wakeful state must be acquired first through long inner exercises that I was here only able to describe in principle. You see, this suppression of all content does not succeed at the first attempt. It has to be practised again and again. In some this will takes years of practice, in others, if they have the right predisposition, it could be months, depending on destiny; and then they succeed in keeping their mind empty without falling asleep, so that the world of spirit can enter them.

Of course—and some may say this—if a person believes he has reached the world of spirit this might be mere self-suggestion. So let us ask: how can we distinguish between self-suggestion and what the spiritual researcher, the initiate, calls a real world of spirit? We can only do so through life itself. Just as in real life we distinguish between a hot iron in our mind from an actual iron by the fact that the mental image of the iron does not burn us but the real iron does, so in the world of spirit we can experience actual realities streaming into our empty consciousness. We simply know the difference, just as we know the difference between a real iron that burns us and one in our mind. Life itself tells us how to discern spiritual reality as opposed to mere self-suggestion.

In the book I referred to [*Knowledge of the Higher Worlds*] I used a term for this second stage of supersensible knowledge—Inspiration—drawn from an old usage that we should not take amiss, for some terminology is needed after all. If we achieve inspired knowledge, we experience ourselves in a sense in a third realm of human nature. First we have our physical being, then our etheric being; and now we experience ourselves in this third being. But as we do so, we not only know ourselves to be independent of our body as in our strengthened, imaginative thinking, but fully outside it. We have reached the condition that we can call living in the spirit outside the physical body. Then we are also able to leave the etheric body—that is, we have eradicated all imaginative content, including, likewise, this life tableau which we first created. This means we have submerged in the unconscious what we have in earthly life, and live now outside of our physical and etheric existence. But when we achieve this, our retrospective gaze reaches back not just to birth or conception but further into the past: we gaze into a world of spirit in which we lived as being of spirit and soul before we descended into the physical world. We perceive ourselves acting and living in this world of spirit, just as we see ourselves as physical human beings in the physical world. We learn to see that what nature develops as our physical embryo must unite with what descends from worlds of spirit, for we now perceive this ourselves. And after gaining this perception, through emerging entirely from our physical and etheric body, we then return to them. The moment of our vision of the world of spirit ends and, re-entering the physical and etheric bodies, we find that this earthly life is a reflection of what we were soul-spiritually before we descended to earth. And in the very act of returning into our body, our physical and etheric body, we develop the strength for what I will call a configured, individualized seership. Having experienced, outside of our physical and etheric body, a more generalized world of spirit which we passed through in pre-earthly existence, when we come back into the physical and etheric bodies—not submerging in them but let us say inhabiting them, dwelling in them—we now learn to distinguish between the spiritual beings of a higher world with whom we were united before we descended to earthly life, just as we distinguish here between different human individuals. We learn to perceive beings who never descend to earth, never assume a physical body: divine, spiritual beings. We inhabit the world of spirit with them before we descend to this earth. And now we learn to perceive, by virtue of our soul and spirit alternating between being outside and within the body, how these higher beings of spirit and soul amongst whom we lived before we came to earth include the human souls who are still waiting to descend to experience earthly life at a later date than we have.

And so, through this stage of inspired knowledge, we learn to perceive the aspect of our eternal being of which very little account is taken by our temporal awareness, even by people of a religious sensibility. In our contemporary world, people don't much care about looking back to pre-earthly existence. They are interested—even if only through some faith or tradition—in what lies beyond death, since this is something that still awaits them. By contrast, since they're alive and here, they don't much feel the need to reflect on what happened before birth. But they are interested in whether and how their life might continue. In their egoism they are interested in the second aspect of eternity: immortality, living on after death. In modern languages we don't even have a word for the other aspect, for pre-earthly existence that stretches out infinitely behind us, as immortality stretches forward. In fact, we only come to perceive the eternal nature of human life when we can turn again to words that ancient languages had for it, roughly speaking 'unbornhood', a term as significant as immortality. Modern initiation science recomposes the eternal nature of the human being again from both unbornhood and immortality. The former, though, does not so much serve our egoism as our real insight. As far as immortality is concerned, people can stay with mere belief or faith. Unbornhood, the certainty that my being is a spiritual entity that existed before my physical body came into being, is something I only come to perceive when I can look upon the unborn nature in me, as well as the immortal [...].

Having departed in this way from our physical and etheric body, and feeling ourselves to be dwelling amongst spiritual beings as previously, in the physical body, amongst physical entities and things, we nevertheless still know ourselves to be a human being, to be a particular I. And we only have to embark on the return journey—this is how we experience it—backwards through time into the world we lived in and passed through before our lives on earth began. But feeling ourselves to be within a world of spirit, outside of our physical and etheric body, we can gaze down upon the world of stars. And these now no longer appear to us as stars but as worlds where higher, and also lower, entities dwell. Wherever our physical eyes would see a star, we now perceive a cosmic sphere of other beings. In our physical body we feel at home on the earth. Now in the world of stars we feel at home in a world of spirit, and just as we speak at the first stage of supersensible knowledge of perception through the etheric body, so now we speak of the astral body since we are now within the spirituality of the world of stars. (Lecture in Paris, 26 May 1924, GA 84, pp. 277–82.)

3. The Schooling of Feelings

The task which esoteric schooling sets itself [...] is to show people the means that enable them to make their feelings and will impulses into ones that are healthy and fruitful for Inspiration. As in all matters of esoteric schooling, we are here concerned with an *intimate* governance and shaping of soul life. We must first acquire certain feelings that we know only to a limited degree in ordinary life. Here I will indicate a few of these. Among the most important is a greater sensitivity to 'true' and 'untrue', to 'right' and 'wrong'. Of course anyone in ordinary life has similar feelings. But an esoteric pupil must develop them to a *far* greater degree. Let us assume that someone makes a logical error: someone sees this and corrects it. And now let us be clear that reasoned judgement plays the major part here, and that a feeling of *pleasure* in what is correct and *displeasure* in what is not is relatively insignificant. I am not saying that there is no pleasure or displeasure at all. But the degree to which they are present in ordinary life must be vastly increased in esoteric schooling. The esoteric pupil must attend systematically to his life of soul, and he must reach a point where something logically incorrect becomes a source of *pain* for him, one no less severe than a physical pain. And likewise what is 'right' or 'correct' must really be a cause of pleasure or joy to him. Where, therefore, someone else would only apply his reasoned judgement, the esoteric pupil must learn to experience the whole range of feelings, from pain through to enthusiasm, from anxious tension through to delighted release in relation to truth. Indeed, he must learn to feel something like hatred for what in a 'normal' person is experienced only as a cold, sober appraisal of something 'incorrect'. He must develop a love of truth in himself, one that bears a very personal character—as warm and personal as a lover feels for his beloved. In scholarly circles, no doubt, we also hear people speaking a great deal of 'love of truth'. But what they mean can in no way be compared with what the esoteric pupil has to undergo in this regard in tranquil inner soul work. Patiently he must repeatedly conjure in his mind this or that 'truth', this or that 'falsehood', and surrender himself to this: not only so as to school his power of judgement, which soberly discriminates between 'true' and 'false', but in order to gain a very personal relationship to all this.

It is certainly true to say that at the beginning of such schooling a person may become oversensitive in this regard. An incorrect judgement that he hears in his proximity, an inconsistency and so on, can cause him really unbearable pain. This must be taken account of during schooling, since otherwise it might pose a grave danger for the pupil's equanimity. If we ensure that our character remains steadfast, then storms can rage in the soul but we retain the strength to live with our surroundings with harmonious countenance and gesture. Certainly it will be wrong for the esoteric pupil to come into conflict with his surroundings so that he finds them unendurable or even seeks to flee them. The higher world of feeling must not develop at the cost of equable activity and work in the outer world. This is why an inner intensification of feeling life must go hand-in-hand with a strengthening of our power of resistance to outward impressions. Practical esoteric schooling therefore always requires that the exercises for schooling of our feeling life are never undertaken without at the same time ensuring that we develop a sense of tolerance in life. We must be able *simultaneously* to feel the keenest pain when, say, someone offers an incorrect judgement and yet be completely tolerant of this person because we have a vivid understanding that he can't help judging in this way, and that his outlook is therefore to be regarded as a *fact*.

The right thing is for the esoteric pupil's inner life to be reshaped increasingly into a dual existence. Ever richer occurrences will unfold within him as he takes his pilgrimage through life, becoming ever more autonomous in contrast with what the outer world presents to him: a second world. But this dual existence will be most beneficial for the way he lives his life. He develops quick and ready discernment and assurance in his resolves. Where someone far removed from such schooling must pursue long sequences of thought, driven hither and thither between decision and indecision, the esoteric pupil will swiftly survey situations, discovering, for instance, circumstances hidden from ordinary view. He will then often require much patience to go along with other people's much slower way of grasping things, whereas for him it happens like lightning.

So far we have only spoken of the qualities that feeling life must acquire so that Inspiration can come about in the right way. The other question is this: how do feelings become fruitful so that they also bear thoughts that really originate from the world of Inspiration? If we wish to understand what answer esoteric science gives to this question, we must realize that the human being's life of soul always possesses a certain store of feelings that exceed what is stimulated in us by sensory perceptions. We feel more, as it were, than outer things compel us to. In ordinary life, this excess is used in a way that must be transformed during esoteric schooling. Consider a feeling of fear or anxiety. It is evident that in many instances the fear is greater than actually corresponds to outer reality. Imagine that an esoteric pupil works energetically on himself so that in no case he encounters does he need to have greater fear and anxiety than is justified by outward events. Now a certain degree of fear or anxiety is always engendered when we engage our inner strength. This inner strength is in fact lost because fear or anxiety arise. The esoteric pupil really does save this inner strength when he forbids himself from feeling fear and other such emotions. It then remains available for something else. If he repeats such occurrences often, this continuous saving of soul powers forms an inner storehouse: the pupil will soon find that these economies of feeling grow into the seeds of thoughts that give expression to revelations of the higher life. This cannot be 'proven' in the ordinary sense. One can only advise the esoteric pupil to do one thing or another; and when he does so he will see that unmistakeable fruits arise.

What has been described here could, to a superficial view, appear contradictory: an enrichment of feelings on the one hand, so that what otherwise arises in only rational judgement here elicits feelings of pleasure, pain and so forth; and on the other hand, *economies* of feeling. This contradiction

immediately vanishes when we consider that these economies should relate to feelings that are stimulated by the
outward senses. What is spared, saved here, appears as an
enrichment in relation to spiritual experiences. And it is
certainly true to say that feelings economized in this way in
relation to the sense-perceptible world not only become
available in the other realm but also prove to be *creative* in
that realm. They create the material for thoughts in which the
world of spirit manifests.

But if it were only a matter of *these* economies, this
would not take us particularly far. More is necessary for
greater success. We must provide the soul with a still
greater store of feeling-engendering strength than is possible by this means. We must, for instance, by way of
experiment, expose ourselves to certain outward impressions, and then entirely deny ourselves the feelings that
would arise in consequence in a so-called 'normal' state.
For instance, we must invoke an event that would 'normally' excite the soul in some way, and entirely forbid such
excitation. This is how we can do so: either by actually
facing such an occurrence or simply picturing it. The latter
is in fact better for esoteric schooling. Since the pupil has
already been initiated into the faculty of Imagination, either
prior to or at the same time as his preparation for Inspiration, he ought really to be able to imaginatively picture an
event as vividly as if it actually occurred. Now if the pupil
repeatedly does this in long, inner endeavour, forbidding
himself from feeling the 'normal' feelings in response, this
will create the fertile ground in him for Inspiration to
develop. (GA 12 (1905–1908), pp. 55–61.)

Now the soul forces stored away within the pupil as an inner treasury because he relinquishes 'normal' feeling responses would certainly transform into inspirations without more ado. And the esoteric pupil would find that true thoughts and pictures rise up in him which embody experiences in the higher worlds. This would begin with the simplest experiences of supersensible occurrences, and gradually more complex and higher realities would surface if the pupil went on working in the direction indicated. But in reality such esoteric schooling would be completely impractical nowadays, and is probably not undertaken wherever people set about working in a serious way. You see, if the pupil sought to develop *everything* that Inspiration can give 'out of himself', he would require immeasurable periods of time to do so—to draw out all the threads of what, here also, we have said about the nature of the human being, about life after death, about humanity's evolution and that of the planet and so forth. It would be like someone endeavouring to draw all geometry out of himself, without heeding what other people have previously found out about it. In theory, of course, this could be done. But it would be foolish to attempt it. In esoteric science we do not do this. Instead we let a teacher tell us about things that inspired predecessors have discovered for humanity, knowledge that has been passed down. Today, this accumulated tradition must provide the foundation for our own Inspiration. The esoteric insights offered in the relevant literature and in lectures etc. can certainly provide this foundation for Inspiration. These include, for instance, teachings about the diverse aspects of human nature (physical body, etheric body, astral body, etc.), knowledge about life after death through to a new incarnation, and then for example everything that has been published about the Akashic Records. While we need Inspiration to discover higher truths and experience them ourselves, we do not need it to understand them. Without Inspiration we cannot first discover the knowledge conveyed in my accounts of reading in the Akashic Records, but if we receive this knowledge, if it is communicated to us, we can gain insight into it through our ordinary logical judgement. No one should assert that I claim things there that cannot be understood without Inspiration. If they are incomprehensible to someone this is not because he does not attain the level of Inspiration, but only because he fails to reflect on them sufficiently.

If such truths are communicated to us, they have a power to evoke Inspiration in the soul. To benefit from such Inspiration one need only receive these insights in a way that is not prosaic and intellectual, and allow the lofty flight of such ideas to engender in us all kinds of feeling experiences. And why should this not happen? Can our feelings remain dull when we survey awesome spiritual occurrences such as the Earth evolving from Moon, Sun and Saturn stages, or gain insight into the infinite depths of human nature and of the etheric and astral body? It would be a terrible shame, would it not, to receive such sublime edifices of thought drily and intellectually? If, when we hear of them, we experience all possible feelings—tension and release, intensification and crisis, progress and reversal, catastrophe and annunciation— then the soil for Inspiration is prepared within us. However, we will only really unfold the necessary life of feeling in response to such communications from a higher world if we undertake exercises of the kind described above. Someone who turns all their powers of feeling towards the outer world of sense perceptions, will regard these accounts of higher worlds as 'arid concepts', as 'grey and theoretical'. He will never be able to understand why another's heart is warmed when he hears the communications of esoteric science. They leave his heart cold. He will even say that all such things are addressed only to the intellect, whereas he is a person of sensibility. He does not realize, however, that it is due to himself that his heart is left cold by such things.

Many still underestimate the power contained and concealed in these communications from a higher world. And consequently they also underestimate the value of our exercises and practices. What use is it, they think, if others tell me what higher worlds are like? I'd like to gain perception of them myself. Mostly such people lack the patience to engage, again and again, with such accounts from higher worlds. If they did so, they would see what kindling power these 'mere tales' have, and how in fact our own Inspiration is awoken when we hear and receive what others have learned through Inspiration. (GA 12 (1905–1908), pp. 63–6.)

Ordinary perception is different from that on the spiritual plane: there we must gather everything to us, must acquire it, must work to, as it were, bring things close to us. A rose we see by the wayside gives us pleasure in this physical world. On the spiritual plane it would not be like this. Nothing resembling a rose on the physical plane would meet us there if we did not strive to enter certain spiritual realms to bring things close to us. What happens here when we *act* is precisely what we have to do in spiritual perception, and vice versa. What is to happen through us is something that we must calmly await in the spiritual domain. Occurrences in the world of spirit only as it were intrude from that world into physical reality: our higher activities are a reflection of spiritual occurrences. And therefore someone who seeks to inwardly understand the truths that are intended to come from spiritual science must increasingly develop two qualities: love of the life of spirit, leading him to active soliciting of the world of spirit (which is also the surest way of all to ensure that we can repeatedly bring these things towards us) and tranquillity, equanimity, a calmness that does not seek success through vanity or ambition but which waits for the grace of receiving Inspiration. Actually being able to wait can be difficult. But one thought that we should keep returning to can help us here. It is hard to grasp because it offends our vanity. This thought is that it doesn't actually matter in the overall scheme of things whether we do something or someone else does. That should not prevent us from doing everything we are obliged to. Nothing should keep us from our duty, but we should avoid frantic hurry and impatience. We all love to be able to do something. A certain resignation is needed to be equally pleased that someone else can do it. We should not love a cause because we ourselves promote it but because it is in the world, whether through us or others. This thought leads us surely to selflessness if we keep harbouring it. Such moods are necessary if we are to live our way in to the world of spirit: not always to explore and investigate ourselves, but equally to understand what others have discovered. (Lecture in Vienna, 3 November 1912, GA 140, pp. 65 f.)

Through Inspiration things spiritually present in our surroundings begin as it were to speak to us: they reveal their being. We do not hear them as voices and tones resembling outward ones, but we hear them spiritually.

Now another form of preparation is needed so that we do not merely hear what unveils our own being to us but come to know a real, objective world. For this we need to enhance a very particular inner virtue. We only become aware of such things through experience. Someone who wishes to attain Inspiration must develop in himself, to a greater degree than necessary in the ordinary world, the virtue of moral courage, of steadfastness, of inner strength. You see, only when we have moral courage and do not withdraw in alarm from something that might possibly endanger us personally will we be able to face up to what speaks to us through Inspiration from spiritual realities. Anyone who has failed to develop sufficient inner courage and moral strength before he enters worlds of spirit will soon see—or rather he won't see this so easily, but others who understand something of these things will notice it—that while certain things in the world of spirit speak to him, this is only an echo of his own being. Because his soul is not strong enough and does not have full self-reliance, it cannot preserve its nature within itself but instead emanates it, and this, the soul's own being, is reflected back to it. A soul not prepared for Inspiration through moral courage will very soon appear as one who hears something like 'voices of the spirit'; but these spiritual voices will be nothing more than what the soul bears within it, an echo merely of its own being. When such a soul recognizes that this is so, it will be greatly downcast by what reaches it from the world of spirit.

And so we see that an important inner quality, one with an intrinsically moral character, must be strengthened and consolidated if a soul seeks to delve upwards into the supersensible world. Moral courage, steadfastness, is required, and is a necessary preparation for real Inspiration. From this it becomes apparent that it is above all necessary for us to strengthen our moral courage in the physical world, already, before trying to become a spiritual investigator, so that the soul can also really perceive through Inspiration the revelations of what is first given through Imagination.

There are a good many who failed to understand this thoroughly enough, who believed they could rely on the soul's moral courage, then gave this soul the means to rise into the supersensible world. But encountering the soul there after a while, it became apparent that this was able only to reflect its own being, which it interpreted as 'tones', as 'words'.

Thus spiritual schooling is intimately connected with the enhancement of moral strength, and this is why every properly communicated spiritual schooling will place such emphasis, above all else, on strengthening and consolidating this. Wherever you find an account of methods for penetrating higher worlds, such as my book *Knowledge of the Higher Worlds*, you will also find there indications of the need to enhance this moral strength. This quality as we find it in ordinary life in the physical world is not yet sufficient; it has to be intensified, enhanced and consolidated. (Lecture in Berlin, 3 April 1913, GA 62, pp. 429–31.)

4. Harnessing the Power of Speech and Inner Silence

Now let us endeavour to develop meditation by dwelling, for instance, on the following: 'Wisdom lives in light.'

This idea cannot derive from sense impressions because in sensory terms it is not the case that wisdom lives in light. In such an instance we hold back thought to an extent that prevents it connecting with the brain. If we develop an inner activity of thinking in this way, one not bound up with the brain, the effect of this meditation on our soul will give us the sense that we are on the right path. In meditative thinking we do not invoke a process of breakdown in our nervous system, and so we never become sleepy in this kind of meditation however long we continue to do it, whereas this can easily happen in our ordinary thinking.

In fact, the opposite often occurs when one meditates. People often complain that they fall asleep the moment they start meditating. This is because they are practising it imperfectly. It is quite natural that when we meditate we first employ the kind of thinking we have always been accustomed to. Only gradually do we learn to quieten ordinary external thinking. Once we have reached this point, meditation will no longer make us sleepy; and thus we will know that we are on the right path.

When the inner power of thinking is developed without us using our external corporeality, we can acquire knowledge of inner life and perceive our true self, our higher I.

We find in this type of meditation just described, which leads to emancipation of the inner power of thinking, the path to true knowledge of the human self. Only through such insight do we come to see that this human self is not bound up within the limits of the physical body. On the contrary, we learn to see that this self is united with the phenomena of the world around us. In ordinary life we see the sun here, and the moon, we see the mountains and there the hills, plants and animals. In this kind of meditation, by contrast, we feel united with everything we see and hear—we become part of it, and for us there is now only an external world, which is our own body. Whereas ordinarily we are here and the outer world is all around us, after developing the independent power of thinking we are outside our body and one with all that we otherwise see; and our body, within which we otherwise dwell, is outside us. We look back upon it, and it has now become the only world upon which we can look from without.

In this way, by liberating the power of thinking, we can really emerge from our physical body and regard it as something external to us. We can go further, though. We can for example give a positive answer to why we wake up each morning. During sleep our physical body lies in bed, and we are in fact outside it, just as is the case in meditative thinking. When we awaken, we return to our physical body, drawn back to it by hundreds and thousands of forces as if by a magnet. Usually people know nothing of this. But when they liberate themselves through meditation they are consciously drawn back by the same power that otherwise unconsciously draws their soul back into their physical body when they wake up.

Through such meditation we also learn how a person descends from higher worlds in which he lived between death and rebirth, and how we unite with the forces and substances passed on to us by parents, grandparents and other forebears. We become acquainted with the powers that between death and rebirth draw people back to a new incarnation.

As an outcome of such meditation, we can look back on a great part of the life which we passed in the world of spirit before birth, before conception, between death and rebirth. Yet through the kind of meditation just described we can usually only look back to a certain point before our latest incarnation, and not further back into former incarnations.

To look back to former incarnations nowadays, as long as the previously mentioned organ has not developed in the human brain, another kind of meditation is required than the meditative thinking that we have just described. This other form can only arise when feeling is introduced into the subject of meditation. The meditant can also imbue with feeling everything we have just described as meditation.

We will now consider this content of meditation which must be permeated by feeling and sensitive perception. If for instance we take the phrase 'Wisdom shines out in the light' and we feel inspired by the radiating wisdom, feel elevated, inwardly warmed through by this meditative content, and if we can dwell in it with enthusiastic feelings, and meditate on this, then there is more before our souls than meditation in thoughts. The strength which we then use inwardly as the power of feeling is the same that we otherwise employ in speech. Speech is brought forth when we penetrate our thoughts with inner feeling, with inner sensitivity. This is how speech originates, and by this means the Broca area is produced in the brain:[15] the thoughts of our inner life, permeated by inner feeling, become active in the brain and in this way develop the organ that is the physical instrument of speech.

When we meditate in this way, when our meditation is really permeated by such feelings, then we retain in our soul the strength we expend in daily life when speaking. We can say that speech is the embodying of our inner strength, which expresses these feeling-imbued thoughts. If instead of allowing our soul strength to emerge in speech we develop meditation out of these feeling-imbued thoughts, and if we keep practising and progressing in this meditation, then we gradually acquire the capacity—even without the physical organ now—to look back into former lives on earth through initiation, and also investigate the period between earthly lives, the span we always spend between one death and the next birth.

By developing this capacity to hold back speech within the soul or, as the esotericist would say, by retaining the 'Word' within the soul, we can look back to the primordial beginning of our earth, to what the Bible calls the act of creation by the Elohim. We can look back to the time when recurring lives on earth began for humanity. You see, the esoteric development we achieve by this means, holding back the Word or speech within us, enables us to see successive eras in so far as they are connected with our earth, with the spiritual life of our planet. We become able to perceive the beings of the higher hierarchies in so far as they are connected with the spiritual life of the earth.

But these two powers of seership, developed in meditation through thoughts and feeling-imbued thoughts, cannot lead us to experiences that occurred prior to the period of our present earth—cannot give us experiences connected with our planet's former embodiments. To delve further into these, a third meditative power is required, which we will now briefly describe.

We can continue by penetrating the content of our meditation with will impulses, doing so for instance by meditating on this phrase, 'The wisdom of the world shines out in the light', in a way that really allows us to feel, without artificially invoking it, the impulse of our will as connected with this activity. We can feel our own being's close affinity with the outstreaming power of light, and can let this light shine and resonate through the world. We must feel the impulse of our will to be connected with this meditation.

If we meditate in this way, so that our meditation is filled with will impulses, we hold back a power that would otherwise pass into the pulsing of our blood. We can easily observe that the life of our inner I can pass over into the blood's pulsation if we remember that we grow pale when we're afraid and red when ashamed. Here we see the soul entering into the pulsing of our blood. When this same power that influences the blood is activated without descending into the blood flow, remaining instead in the soul alone, this third form of meditation begins as one we can influence through impulses of will.

Someone who undertakes these three forms of esoteric development feels firstly, when he emancipates the power of thinking, as if he had an organ at the root of his nose. This organ is described as a lotus flower, and through it he can discern this I or self extending far into space.

Secondly, when he has developed feeling-imbued thoughts through meditation, this strength that would otherwise have become speech gradually makes him aware of what is called the 16-petalled lotus in the region of the larynx. With the aid of this lotus he can understand what is connected with temporal things from the beginning of the earth through to its end. By means of this organ we also learn to perceive the reality of the occult meaning of the Mystery of Golgotha [...].

By holding back the soul strength that in ordinary everyday life would reach into the blood and its pulsation, an organ is developed in the region of the heart that I describe in my book *Occult Science*. By means of this we come to understand the greater span of evolution which is known in esotericism as Saturn, Sun and Moon, the former incarnations of our earth. (Lecture in London, 1 May 1913, GA 152, pp. 25–30.)

Just as the power of thinking as an activity of spirit and soul can be sundered from the physical body in this kind of spiritual chemistry, so another power which we otherwise only use bodily, which as it were pours into the body, can be separated out from it. However strange this sounds, this other power is that of speech, a power we otherwise use when we speak.

What happens when we speak? Our thoughts live in us, our thoughts let our brain resonate with them; this has a connection with our organs of speech. Muscles are set in motion and what we experience inwardly flows out into our words and lives in them. From the point of view of spiritual science, we have to say that in speech we pour what lives in our soul into the body's physical organs. By sharpening our attention, as described, and adding something further to it—once again, an activity that is usually already present but must become infinitely enhanced—the power of speech is detached from the body and physical senses. This power is devotion.

We know this at moments when we have religious feelings, when we are surrendered to this or that being with love, when we can follow things and their laws in rigorous enquiry, when we can forget ourselves with all our feelings and thoughts. We know this devotion and surrender. Really it flows only between the lines of ordinary life. The spiritual scientist must endlessly enhance and strengthen this power. He must indeed be given up to the stream of existence in a way that he is otherwise given up only in profound sleep, without himself doing anything, adding anything to what he experiences. In sleep our limbs rest and all senses are silenced. We are surrendered to this state and do nothing—but in sleep we are unconscious. If, however, we can repeatedly suppress all sensory activity by inner intention, can suppress all limb activity and place our physical, sensory life in a state known otherwise only in deep sleep, and yet remain awake, fully maintaining our bright inner awareness and developing the feeling of being poured into the stream of existence, wanting nothing other than whatever the world wishes for us, then—invoking it in a form distinct and separate from the practice of attention—the soul will grow ever stronger. We must repeatedly try to invoke this feeling.

Now these two exercises, that of sharpening attention and that of surrender and devotion, must be practised separately from each other since they are contraries. Where attentiveness requires the greatest harnessing of forces, deep concentration on the object of meditation, devotion requires our passive surrender to the stream of existence, immeasurable enhancement of that feeling we find in religious experience or in other devotion to a beloved being. The fruits we gain from such immeasurable enhancement and attentiveness mean that we separate our soul-spiritual life from corporeal life. And so the vigour that otherwise pours into words, that is always active and never stays still, that sets the nerves in motion, can be separated from the outward motions of speech and then rests within itself in the realm of soul and spirit. Here the power of speech as we can call it is sundered from its physical, sensory existence, and we experience what, to use Goethe's phrase, we can call spiritual hearing.

Here, once again, we experience ourselves outside of the body, but now we are submerged in things and perceive their inner reality. We perceive them, though, so that we echo or recreate them within ourselves, as in an inner gesture—not simply like a facial expression but a kind of inner gesture. The soul and spirit sundered from the body seek to express our preoccupation in a gesture, as if drawing on a heightened talent for imitation. What otherwise only arises in someone with a special disposition and talent for imitation is now performed by the soul sundered from the body, and this enables it to perceive. The soul submerges itself in things, and actively recreates the powers at play there. All this perceiving in the world of spirit depends on activity: by observing the activity we have to engage in to recreate the intrinsic flux and nature of things, we also perceive them. In the ordinary outer world hearing is passive: we listen. In spiritual hearing, speaking and listening flow as it were together: we submerge ourselves in the nature of things and hear their inner activity. What Pythagoras called the music of the spheres is something that the spiritual scientist can really experience. He immerses himself in the things and beings of the world of spirit and hears by speaking. A speaking hearing, a hearing speech as we immerse ourselves in the reality of things, is what we experience here. And this gives rise to true Inspiration. (Lecture in Vienna, 6 April 1914, GA 153, pp. 19–22.)

Having once gained this ability to experience ourselves in the etheric, to experience the etheric world with and through ourselves, we can progress to a different mode of schooling our soul forces. This involves activating in the soul the opposite process, we can say, from what was first described. First we attempted to make our thinking very inwardly active, very vivid and vital, thus acquiring within us not passive thinking but an inwardly vibrant streaming, pulsing, weaving and surging. Now we have to try to suppress again, with the same inner intent and power of will, what we first activated in the soul as freely floating thoughts in the soul.

In the soul exercises I'm intent on, everything I'm describing must be undertaken in the way a mathematician sets to work to solve his problems—most deliberately, without any false mysticism, fantasy, let alone anything like autosuggestion. We must undertake these inner exercises with the same sober coolness with which we solve geometric problems—for warmth and enthusiasm arise through what we then perceive and not through the method itself. Nevertheless, one thing becomes apparent: when we succeed in having this empowered thinking, developed especially, say, where we picture our life so far in thoughts that can entirely absorb us if we try to dwell on them, it is then hard to get free of them again. But we have to develop in ourselves the strength to suppress these thoughts again, just as we can invoke them first through our own activity. In other words, we must become able to extinguish all the thoughts in our mind having first very actively kindled them. Extinguishing our ordinary thoughts is hard enough, but still relatively easy compared with extinguishing thoughts that we have first placed in our awareness through intense activity.

That is also why this extinguishing signifies something quite different. And if we succeed, through long practice once again—though we can undertake these exercises at the same time as the others so that both capacities develop at the same time—to engender vigorous, active processes of thinking but then also erase them again from the mind, then something overshadows the soul which, since we need words to describe it, I will call 'the soul falling inwardly silent'.

This inner silence is something we simply do not have in the ordinary mind. The first thing the spiritual researcher needs if he seeks to pursue the anthroposophic path of spiritual enquiry is a strengthened life of thinking and picturing, by means of which he develops self-knowledge in the way I have described. The other thing he must school is an entirely empty mind, so that everything living in the soul as thinking, feeling and will falls silent, though only after he has intensively enhanced these soul faculties. Then this inner silence in the soul is something very special. And I can describe this, the second stage of spirit cognition, roughly in the following way.

Let us imagine that we are in a large city where a terrible tumult is going on. We are deafened by it. We leave the city and, after walking for a while, we can still hear the noises behind us, the clanging and blaring, though it has grown quieter. The further we walk, the quieter it becomes. When we finally arrive in the quiet of the wood we find tranquillity all around us: thus we have taken a journey that led us all the way from thundering tumult to outward silence. But I can continue the journey, as it were, into greater and greater stillness. This does not happen in external reality, but the idea becomes very real when we arrive at what I have called the soul falling silent.

I would like to use a very trivial comparison: we may have a certain capital, and spend more and more of it. We have ever less, and eventually none at all. Then we have zero assets. But we can go still further and accrue debts. Then we have less than nothing. We're in the red. We know this in mathematics—less than nothing as a quantity. The same can happen with tranquillity, with silence. Compared with the noise of the world we can regard complete outer silence as zero. But then we can go further and make it stiller than still, negative silence, negative peace. And thus when we extinguish this strengthened soul life it becomes still quieter, calmer than what I will call merely 'zero' quiet. In the soul is created a tranquillity that is more than the mere silence and tranquillity of the ordinary mind.

And when we have worked our way through to this silence, when the soul feels that it has removed itself from the world, not only by ensuring that the world has fallen quiet around it—for the world as such can only attain a zero degree of quiet—but through the soul finding a deeper silence than the world's silence, then, in this deepening, negative silence the world of spirit begins to speak to us from the other side of existence, really to speak. Otherwise, when we speak with words formed outwardly in the air we interrupt the world's stillness and tranquillity. By creating in ourselves this quiet that is deeper than zero quiet, deeper than mere silence, something starts to speak to us from the world of spirit, though this is a language we first have to become accustomed to, that in no way resembles the language of words. This other language to which we gradually become accustomed approaches us in terms that we already know from the sense world, in colours, tones and so forth. Based on these familiar sense experiences we can begin to describe the different impressions made on us by the world of spirit.

I would like to draw your attention to certain details here. Let us assume that in this inward silence of the soul we have experienced something that makes the following impression on us: from depths of spirit something is now present that comes towards us aggressively, we might say—acts upon us in a somewhat arousing way. Initially this is a spiritual experience: we know that spirit is manifesting. Now we compare what we experience in this way with something we witness in the world of the senses, and then we discover this: the corresponding experience we have in the sensory world is roughly that of the colour yellow. Just as we coin a phrase to express something in the sense world, so now we employ the colour yellow to express this spiritual experience. We use language to express sensory realities, and in the same way we use sensory qualities, sense impressions to describe what we receive from the world of spirit in a spiritual way in the deep silence of the soul.

And thus we describe the world of spirit. I described it in this way in my books *Theosophy* and *Occult Science*. We just have to understand such accounts in the right way. We have to understand that a new language arises in response to the soul's silence. In our outward, articulated speech we speak out into the world as human beings whereas now something resounds into us from the world of spirit which we must in a sense reproduce in tangible words. It can only be perceived with the necessary subtlety and must then be translated into human language if we wish to express it in words that are of course drawn from the world of sense perception.

And in this way, experiencing what comes to us in the soul's silence, we can come to see that the world of strengthened thinking we first discovered is basically only a picture of what we can now perceive, and for which we only now have a language—a picture which was our point of departure for penetrating the silence of the soul. Now the world of spirit speaks to us through the soul's silence. And now too we become able to extinguish again this whole tableau of our life which we first formed, which was etherically conjured before us by earthly life; and in this way the soul's inner silence arises in contrast to our own life as we lead it on earth. The illusion of the ego that can live only by means of the physical body now ceases.

Someone who holds too strongly to his ego through an egoism either theoretical or realized will be unable to create this soul silence in response to his own life tableau. If we wrestle with theoretical and practical egoism, we come to see that initially we have this ego by virtue of the body that serves us in physical life; the body enables us to say 'I' to ourselves. If we depart from this bodily sense of I sufficiently to enter into what I described as the etheric world, so that we flow together with the world that is one with our own etheric, then we no longer hold so fast to this ego; and then we experience what this life tableau we have risen to is an image of: we experience our pre-earthly existence. We experience this pre-earthly existence in a world of spirit in which we lived before we descended into a physical human body through conception and birth. (Lecture in Basel, 9 April 1923, GA 84, pp. 24–9.)

But when we really experience this profound silence of the soul, then there arises from it everything that surrounds us as spiritual realities. Inspiration comes fully into its own in us.

And having experienced this profound soul silence, we become able actually to hear spiritually what lives in the world of spirit. The ordinary sense world becomes a means for us to hint at what lives in this spiritual world. I would like to speak very tangibly of real spiritual perception. Out of this deep silence of the soul resounds something that seems to thrill or to stir me, to come towards me with a certain vivacity. This is something that makes an impression on me that resembles the effect of the colour yellow if I am sensitive to it. And thus I have something in the world of senses which I can employ to express what I have experienced in the world of spirit. I express my perception by saying that it affects me as the colour yellow does, or like the tone C or C sharp, or like warmth or cold. Thus what I experience in sensory reality becomes material I can draw on to describe, in ordinary words, what appears to me in the world of spirit. In this way the whole sense world becomes something like a language to express what I experience in the world of spirit. Those who try to make too rapid progress do not understand this, and get no further than a superficial view of these things. The spiritual enquirer encounters an experience that makes the same impression on him as colours in the sense world, and this is why he describes his spiritual experiences in terms of colours, tones and so forth. Just as we should not confuse the word 'table' with an actual table, so likewise we should not confuse the signifiers we use to describe the spiritual world with that world itself, which springs forth from the soul's deep silence.

Having reached this place, we arrive at the point of extinguishing this whole life tableau which we first conjured before us. We invoke empty consciousness not only in relation to particular ideas and thoughts but towards the whole of our earthly life, specifically in its inward form. In a sense we extinguish ourselves as earthly human being. But by virtue of our ability to extinguish the earthly self bound up with our physical body and thereby to experience the soul's deep silence, we discover what we had become as human spirit and soul before we descended from the world of spirit and clothed ourselves in a physical body. Out of the deep silence of the soul we experience the spirit and soul that we were in pre-earthly existence. And just as we found our way into our physical surroundings in our physical body, so now, by transposing ourselves into what we were in the world of spirit and soul, we come to perceive that in this pre-earthly existence we lived in the vicinity of beings of soul and spirit, and that we were one among them, of the same nature as them. We penetrate into that world of spirit, have full vision of the realm from which we descended into earthly existence. (Lecture in Prague, 27 April 1923, GA 84, pp. 169–71.)

The cosmos itself and our own true being as it existed before birth, before this life on earth, only come to us through Inspiration, when the world of spirit streams into us from without. And when we succeed in creating an empty mind in this way our soul is filled initially by mere wakefulness, and within this state we must be able to come to a certain inner stillness, inner tranquillity. I can only describe this tranquillity in the following way.

Imagine you're in a very noisy city, surrounded by the roar of traffic. It can be awful to be right in the midst of such a racket. Imagine you're in a big, modern capital, London say. But now imagine that you walk away from the city and gradually leave it behind you, so that the noise slowly subsides. Try to really imagine the noise fading as you get further and further away from the city. It becomes quieter and quieter. At last, let us say, you reach a wood where all is quiet and still, where all is silent around you. You have, in a sense, reached the zero point of the audible.

But you can keep going. And here I will use a rather trivial comparison to show what I mean by this. Imagine you have money in your wallet and that you keep spending it day after day. The money grows less, just as the noise did. And at last a day comes when there's nothing left in your wallet. We can compare this 'nothing' with the zero point of noiselessness. But what do we do if we wish to keep eating? We get into debt. I'm not recommending this particularly, but I'm using it as a comparison. How much do we then have in our wallet, as it were? Less than nothing. And the more debt we accrue, the greater our less-than-nothing becomes.

Now imagine that the same is true of stillness—that we can go beyond absolute quiet, the zero point of noiselessness, and enter the negative of hearing, stiller than still, more silent than silence. This must in fact happen if we are to succeed, through intensified activity, in creating this inner tranquillity and silence as I described yesterday. But when we arrive at this inner, negative audibility, this quiet that is greater than zero quiet, then we are in the world of spirit in a way that enables us to hear and not only see it. Then what we previously perceived is enhanced through the quality of tone to become a more living world. Then we stand within the real world of spirit and have in a sense reached the further shore of existence at those moments when we cross over. On this further shore the ordinary sense world vanishes and we find ourselves in the world of spirit. But we must [. . .] be properly prepared for this so that we can also return at any moment. But something else occurs as well: an experience that we could never previously have had. What I described as an inwardly fully experienced, comprehensive, let us say cosmic, feeling of happiness transforms at this moment when we create an empty mind through tranquillity into an equally comprehensive soul pain, soul suffering. And we discover that the world is founded on cosmic pain, or on a cosmic element that we can only experience in pain. By penetrating this experience, so gladly despised by a humanity seeking outward happiness, we become acquainted with the truth that all existence must ultimately be born from pain. And having penetrated, through the insight granted by initiation, to this cosmic experience of pain we can then say the following out of real inner knowledge:

If we consider our eyes, which reveal to us in the physical world the glories of this world, granting us nine-tenths of what fills our lives in physical existence between birth and death, we find they are embedded in a cavity which in fact originally evolved as a vulnerability, an injury to the body. If the body today suffers a wound that forms a cavity in it, we can see this as the same thing that our eyes originated from. External accounts of evolution strike a far too neutral and indifferent tone. Even in purely physical terms, what led to the eye cavities being created by external penetration occurred at a time when we were still unconscious beings. It was an occurrence which, if raised into consciousness, would have signified a painful injury to the organism. In fact, the whole human organism was born from an element which, if we experienced it with the awareness we possess today, would be an experience of pain. And at this stage of knowledge we can gain a profound sense of how all happiness, all pleasure, all blessedness in this world, emerges from the ground of pain, an element like the soil from which the plant emerges, which also really always signifies pain.

If we human beings could be transformed in an instant into

the substance of the earth and yet retain our conscious mind, this would lead to an infinite intensification of our feelings of pain. This reality, which reveals itself from the world of spirit, is one to which shallower natures respond by saying that God is surely not like this; that God, they think, is so mighty that he can bring forth everything from joy. For them that is a much more palatable prospect. (Lecture in Penmaenmawr, 20 August 1923, GA 227, pp. 54–7.)

The world into which we enter in this way as we proceed beyond Imagination into the stillness of existence—from which the world of spirit emerges and announces itself as I described, shining in colours and sounding in tones—is substantially different from the one we perceive through our senses. And when we live within this spiritual world, as we must if it is to be available to us, then we notice that all sensory, physical things and processes have in fact arisen from this world of spirit. As earthly human beings we really only see half the world. The other half is hidden from us, remains 'occult'. Yet it shines through every crack: in every occurrence in the physical sense world, spiritual reality holds sway, initially in imaginative pictures and then in what this reality can itself creatively grant us in Inspiration. We can come to be at home in this world of Inspiration, and then we will discover there the origins of all earthly things, all earthly creations. We discover there, as I already suggested, our own pre-earthly existence. In line with older traditions I have called this world, which lies beyond what we perceive through Imagination, the 'astral'. The name doesn't matter but we need some kind of terminology. And what we ourselves bear within us of this world, which we brought with us into physical and etheric existence, can accordingly be called the human astral body. It encloses within it, in a sense, our actual I organization. And so to higher perception it becomes apparent that the human being is fourfold, consisting of a physical body, an etheric body or body of formative forces, an astral body and an I organization. But we can only approach this I organization through a further step in supersensible cognition, one to which I referred in my books, especially, *Knowledge of the Higher Worlds*, as that of Intuition. (Lecture in Penmaenmawr, 20 August 1923, GA 227, pp. 54–7.)

5. Inspiration and the Perception of Nature

If we wish to understand the whole nature of Inspiration we must now impress on ourselves a further distinctive fact. You see, for someone who approaches Inspiration there is no difference between an objective law of nature and what he experiences within his soul as thought. He finds that a law of nature belongs to him just as much as what lives within his soul. Let me put it like this. When someone upon whom Inspiration dawns decides to do something, out of some motive or other, this is founded on lawfulness. Such lawfulness is one he will initially experience as living in his own breast, as peculiar to himself. And yet it is felt to have the same objectivity as can be experienced in the lawfulness of sunrise. We can also see it thus. If I pick up a clock, I feel this to be a matter concerning myself on the physical plane. In terms of physical perception I do not regard sunrise in the same way. But the impulse of the world of Inspiration gives me the sense that what occurs in nature likewise belongs to me.

Here human interest really does expand to encompass natural phenomena, which become our own concerns and interests. As long as we do not experience the life of the plant as intimately as the experiences of our own heart, there can be no truth in Inspiration. Until we can feel a falling stone splashing on the water's surface and making a spray of droplets in the same way as we experience what occurs within our own being, Inspiration will not correspond to the truth.

Another way of putting it is to say that everything in us that we feel to be closer to ourselves than nature's wealth and fullness does not belong to the truths of Inspiration. However, it would be complete nonsense to think that an inspired person would experience someone denting his skull with the same objectivity as a volcanic eruption. Naturally he does make a subjective distinction between these two things. But at the moment someone dents his skull, he won't be in the inspired state. Yet everything that falls within the realm of Inspiration expands his interest over all of nature. In the lecture series I gave in The Hague [GA 145], I pointed out that expanded cognition in general relies on broadened interest. No one can approach the condition of Inspiration without being able to free himself for a brief period at least from things that pertain only to him. He must not always do this of course. On the contrary, he will do well to make a clear distinction between his own concerns and interests and what should be the object of his Inspiration. But if a person expands his interests into objectivity, for instance trying to feel the life of the plant and its growth in the same way as what occurs in his own life, and when what sprouts and grows in the outer world, what develops and fades, is as intimate and familiar to him as the life within himself, then he will be inspired in regard to all that approaches him in this way.

But this kind of interest is inevitably connected with a gradual ascent to a view of the human being such as Goethe gradually developed. Through his efforts [to develop living thoughts], Goethe learned to distinguish human activities from the human entity as such. And this is of really extraordinary importance! What we do or have done belongs to the objective world, is karma realized, whereas what or who we are as personalities is in continual development. The judgement we make about something a person has done must really be written on a quite different sheet from the judgement we make about his intrinsic value. If we wish to approach higher worlds, we must learn to view the human individual with as much objectivity as we bring to bear on a stone or a plant. We must learn to have sympathy also for those who do deeds that we may be compelled to condemn. This separation of a person from his deeds, separation of him also from his karma, is something we must accomplish if we wish to gain the right relationship to higher worlds. (Lecture in Dornach, 20 September 1915, GA 164, pp. 71–3.)

Goethe, for instance, in his mature period, sought to present occurrences between people as natural occurrences. Naturally not as if there were some mechanical necessity in human interplay equivalent to that in natural phenomena—there can be no such thing. Instead, the soul's stance towards occurrences in human life gradually becomes one in which we can regard events in life, between people, with the same objective love with which we observe natural phenomena. This gives rise to the inner tolerance that proceeds from knowledge itself.

And by this means we acquire the ability gradually to let flow into knowledge what must otherwise never flow into it: that is, the terminology originating in feeling and will. On a previous occasion, when I was describing psychoanalysis,[16] we concluded one day with a damning verdict on it, though only after showing this to be intrinsic to the very nature of the subject. And why could we make this verdict? Here a subjective note may be permissible. How could I allow myself to express a seemingly very subjective view of psychoanalysis? This was because I endeavoured—and this is subjective but it may make it easier to understand—to study psychoanalysis in the same way I would study something that I find very pleasant and agreeable. That is, to bring the same objective love to bear on something, whatever its nature, and this is something we must gradually wrestle our way through to. Otherwise in our search for knowledge we are really seeking nothing other than sensation, seeking only what is pleasant in knowledge. And yet we never possess knowledge if we seek only what is agreeable in it!

For our physical life, solar quality never enters our human awareness other than by giving us pleasure or displeasure. From this solar quality only feelings enter, and we must go to meet it with our understanding, delving down into what is otherwise alien to us. We saw that lunar quality has a human affinity, whereas solar quality no longer does. We must carry our understanding down into regions which we do not otherwise penetrate when seeking to bring the solar quality of Inspiration towards us.

True perception of the higher worlds in fact requires preparation in our whole mood of soul, and without this, we cannot enter higher worlds. By this I do not only mean enter them clairvoyantly but also bring understanding to bear on what we find there. The things recounted in *Occult Science* cannot be understood if one seeks to absorb them with the same outlook that we bring to bear on something outwardly neutral, something in mathematics, say. We can only absorb them if we have prepared our sensibility in the right way. Someone who tries to assimilate inspired knowledge with the ordinary understanding of the physical plane resembles a person who imagines he could creep inside a plant and dwell within its life. This is why efforts have always been made to properly prepare people before communicating knowledge of higher worlds to them: slowly preparing them so as to engender the mood of soul that allows this knowledge of higher worlds to act in the right way on their sensibility. You see, the distinctive manner in which one must relate to the higher world does require a certain exertion of our sensibility, a certain coherence, a harnessing of inner powers of soul; it requires above all that we are willing to exert ourselves to some degree in order to find the right relationship to perception of higher worlds, and are not surprised at the need for such effort. (Lecture in Dornach, 20 September 1915, GA 164, pp. 76–8.)

Today I spoke to you about Inspiration. I showed how Inspiration leads us back to our ancient solar condition and estate. But on Old Sun the human being had reached the stage of breathing. That is, what we now know as breathing, which lives in the element of air, had been laid down in us as predisposition. There must therefore be a connection between human breathing and Inspiration. You need only consider the original meaning of the word itself, which expresses the intimate affinity between the breath and 'Inspiration'. Basically, it signifies inhalation. Those who wish to deny the reality of spirit beings would need only to consider the development of language. We have spoken of this previously from a different angle. We can discern the workings of the spirits of language, and discover too how they work within human nature. Then we will find ourselves to be embedded in spirit worlds, and see how spirits work with us, as they do in all that we accomplish in life. And in a very real and tangible way we will then feel our self enlarged, expanded into the greater self of the world. What is otherwise only theoretical will become first-hand feeling. And that is the path to follow in order truly to enter worlds of spirit. (Lecture in Dornach, 20 September 1915, GA 164, p. 84.)

Developing the capacity to live a second existence in our life of thinking by allowing thoughts to live intensely in our mind is still something that remains enclosed within our spatially defined body. Besides this, we can also live outside the body when we learn, through systematic practice, to remove these thoughts from the mind again; and in doing this we acquire an experiential state outside the body. Let me offer a simple exercise for practising this.

Imagine you are looking at a crystal. In other words, your eyes enable you to have it there before you. Someone who seeks a merely mediumistic relationship to it, or a sort of hypnotic condition, simply stares at the crystal so that the impression it makes on him transports him into an unreflective state. Anthroposophic spiritual science has nothing to do with this, but instead has to develop quite different practices. These are concerned ultimately with abstracting from or looking beyond the crystal, in the same way that one otherwise only develops abstract thoughts. So we have a crystal there in front of us and we learn not only to perceive it and understand it physically but to encompass it inwardly too, no longer using our eyes to stare at it, despite having them wide open, and instead shaping our inward perception so that the crystal is no longer there before us. We remove it from our beholding. We can do this exercise also by removing a colour from our vision, so that we no longer see it despite having it in front of us.

And thus we can especially undertake exercises that aim to remove, extinguish thoughts that arise in outward life and in the present moment, or that surface as memories of earlier experiences in our life. We make our mind empty of them so that we are merely awake, alert, but have nothing of the outer world in our mind.

If one does such exercises one discovers in oneself the ability no longer to remain within the confines of one's spatial body but to depart from it. Then we can experience the life of our whole surroundings, otherwise only perceived as sense phenomena.

By this means something occurs in a fully reflective and conscious state that I can compare with a memory of the life we spend in sleep, from falling asleep to awakening. In ordinary sense perception we are confined to the present moment, and in ordinary life, similarly, we are confined to what we have experienced in a waking state.

When you think back on your life, the times you spent asleep are of no concern, are void in your ordinary mind. What the soul experienced during sleep does not appear in your memory. And so our memory is always an interrupted stream, although we overlook this fact.

But what the soul experiences whenever we sleep surfaces

as an intense memory in the condition of awakened consciousness in which we live outside our body. This gives rise to the second stage of perception of supersensible worlds, in which, initially, we can become aware of what we experience as soul whenever our body, our physical body, rests in sleep, tranquil and as if soulless, without sense perception, without expressions of will. In ordinary daily life we can by this means recall what we have experienced each time we were outside our body during sleep. But we must also be clear of the need to properly evaluate what surfaces in this way. We learn to see that what the soul experiences during sleep is an out-of-body experience, and that we only observe this if we can develop a consciousness, a state of existence outside the body. And now we become acquainted not only with something in a sense illumined by an inner light—with our own temporal body, as I described—but now, as we remember back in waking memory that has risen to this exact clairvoyance of a higher kind, we see what we actually experience each time we sleep. This experience is initially somewhat astounding. Just as we live in our ordinary consciousness in daily life in our physical body, and have within us lungs, heart and so forth, so during sleep we do not have a personal human consciousness but a cosmic consciousness. However paradoxical this sounds, supersensible vision perceives that in this awareness it seems as if we were living in replicas of the worlds of planets and stars. We feel ourselves to be within the universal life of the cosmos. In a sense we look upon the world from the perspective of the universal life in the cosmos. (Lecture in London, 17 November 1922, GA 218, pp. 188–90.)

6. The Nature of Inspiration

The world of Imagination is a restless place. It is pervaded by movement, transformation, and nothing comes to rest there. We only find points of tranquillity when we develop beyond the stage of imaginative perception to what can be called 'knowledge through Inspiration'. When seeking knowledge of the supersensible world, it is not necessary firstly to acquire and encompass the full scope of imaginative perception, and only then proceed to 'Inspiration'. Our practice can be arranged so that these things go hand-in-hand, the exercises leading to Imagination and those to Inspiration. After practising these exercises for long enough, we can enter a higher world in which we do not merely perceive but in which we can also orientate ourselves, and which we can interpret. But usually, as we progress, we first discern some phenomena of the imaginative world and after a while gain the sense that we also now begin to find our orientation. Nevertheless, the world of Inspiration is something quite new compared to mere Imagination. Through the former we perceive the transformation of one occurrence into another while through the latter we learn to perceive the inner attributes of transforming *beings*. Through Imagination we perceive the soul expression of beings and entities, whereas through Inspiration we penetrate into their inner, spiritual being. Above all we perceive a multiplicity of spiritual beings and interrelationships between them. In the physical sense world, too, we find a multiplicity of beings and creatures. In the world of Inspiration, this multiplicity is however different in character. There each being has quite specific relationships with others—not, as in the physical world, through outward reciprocal effects but through their inner nature. When we perceive a being in the inspired world, we do not find it exerting any external influence on others comparable to interactions in the physical world, but instead their interrelationship arises through the inner nature of each. This kind of relationship can be compared with the relationship between the separate letters of a word. If we take a word such as 'man', it exists by virtue of the accord of its sounds: m-a-n. Rather than the 'm' acting on and influencing the 'a', both sounds work together, within the whole, through their inner nature. Our observation of the world of Inspiration can therefore be compared with *reading*; and the beings in this world act on the observer like letters that he must become acquainted with, and whose interrelationships he must decipher like a supersensible script. Spiritual science therefore regards perception and knowledge gained through Inspiration as a 'reading of the hidden script'.

We will now clarify how we come to read this 'hidden script', and how what we read can be communicated, by reference to preceding chapters of this very book [*Occult Science*]. We first described the nature of the human being, and how it is composed of diverse aspects. Then we described how the cosmic entity, the planet on which we evolve, passes through various conditions—those of Saturn, Sun, Moon and Earth. The perceptions through which we discern these aspects of the human being on the one hand, and the successive stages of the planet and its previous transformations on the other, become available through imaginative cognition. But now we must also perceive the relationships existing between the Saturn condition and our physical human body, the Sun condition and our etheric body, and so forth. We have to show that the germ of the physical human body arose during the Saturn condition and then developed further towards its present form during the Sun, Moon and Earth stages. We also had to show, for instance, what changes the human being underwent as a result of the sun, and then similarly the moon, separating from the earth. We also had to describe what influences came together to enable the changes in humanity to occur as these manifested during the Atlantean period and in succeeding periods in ancient India, ancient Persia, Egypt and so forth. Our account of these circumstances does not arise from imaginative perception but from the knowledge gained through Inspiration, from a reading of the hidden script. For this kind of 'reading', imaginative perceptions are like the separate letters or phonemes. Yet besides this reading being necessary for deeper elucidation such as described, we could not even understand a person's whole biography if we only saw it in terms of imaginative cognition. While we could perceive how the soul-spiritual aspects of a human being are released at death from what remains in the physical world, without finding proper orientation within our imaginative perceptions we would fail to grasp what happens to a person after death and how preceding states are related to succeeding ones. Without knowledge gained through Inspiration, the imaginative world would remain like a script that we stare at but cannot decipher.

When the spiritual pupil advances from Imagination to Inspiration, it soon becomes apparent how wrong it would be to relinquish understanding of the great panoramas of world phenomena and wish to confine oneself to facts that concern only our immediate interests as human beings. Someone who has not been initiated into these things might well say this: 'It seems important to me only to learn of the fate of the human soul after death. If someone will tell me about this, that will be enough. Why does spiritual science present me with such far-fetched things as conditions on ancient Saturn and Sun, with the departure of the sun and the moon?' But a proper awareness of these matters will show us that the knowledge we seek can never be gained without understanding also of what might appear so unnecessary to us. An account of the states we enter into after death remains incomprehensible and worthless if we cannot connect them with concepts originating in these 'far-fetched' matters. The simplest observation made by a person with supersensible perception necessitates his acquaintance with such things. When, for instance, a plant passes from flowering to fruiting, the supersensible observer sees a transformation occurring in an astral entity which, during flowering, has been covering and enveloping the plant from above like a cloud. If fertilization had not occurred, this astral entity would have assumed a quite different form from the one it now has. And we can understand the whole process perceived through supersensible observation if we have learned to understand our own nature and being through the great world occurrences that happened with the earth and all its inhabitants at the time the sun departed. Prior to fertilization, the plant is in a condition in which the whole earth was before this departure of the sun. After fertilization, the plant's blossom now appears as the earth was when the sun had separated from it but the moon forces were still present. If we can fully internalize the ideas we can gain from knowledge of the sun's departure, we can interpret and perceive the process of plant fertilization in terms of a sun condition prior to fertilization, and a moon condition afterwards. You see, it really is the case that even the smallest occurrence in the world can only be grasped if we see it as a reflection of great world processes. Otherwise its reality remains as incomprehensible to us as a Raphael Madonna for someone who sees only a small blue corner of it while the rest is covered up. Everything that occurs in and around us is a reflection of the great world processes that are connected with our existence. If we wish to grasp what supersensible consciousness shows us of occurrences between birth and death, and again between death and rebirth, we can do so by acquiring the ability to decipher these imaginative perceptions in terms of ideas we have assimilated by contemplating great world processes. It is this contemplation that provides us with the key to understanding human life. And that is why perception of Saturn, Sun and Moon stages of evolution in spiritual science are at the same time a perception of the human being himself.

Through Inspiration we come to the point of perceiving the connections and relationships between beings of the higher world. (GA 13 (1910), pp. 351–7.)

When we proceed far enough in imaginative perception to stand within the outer world of spirit and soul, and have initially succeeded in perceiving our own life tableau, that is, the etheric body or body of formative forces, then we have undergone a certain alteration, a transformation of our cognition. What we accomplish when we perceive this etheric nature is both similar to and yet also very dissimilar from artistic activity, as opposed to the ordinary naturalistic and abstract mode of knowledge. We have to develop a shaping and configuring thinking which is in certain respects reminiscent of the distinctive way in which an artist remembers. Yet on the other hand it is also very different from the mode in which an artist thinks. You see, what an artist forms remains within the realm of imaginative fantasy. This pictorial fantasy is very much bound up with the body, is not liberated from the body. By contrast, the activity we exercise in supersensible imaginative perception is free of our corporeality, and for this reason it also encompasses something real. The artist's creations do not have a reality that could exist fully in the world. The *Venus de Milo*, for instance, is not something you could expect to get up and start walking towards you. What the artist creates is not yet reality in this sense. Similarly, if you look at a painting of a devil you won't be alarmed that it might leap out from the picture to get you. The way in which the artist engages with reality is still bound up with human physical reality, does not yet enter soul-spiritual reality. By contrast, what we acquire in imaginative perception partakes of true reality, of actual occurrence.

It might however be said that, logically and theoretically, cognition in general should not encroach on the domain of artistic activity. This is because cognition means taking a logical succession of steps that link one concept to another in a logical progression. When we move into the realm of art, we step beyond the permitted scope of such knowledge. We could philosophize a long, long time about what the nature of knowledge should be; but if nature, if the world is an artist, it will not surrender its secrets to merely logical enquiry. It withdraws from merely logical investigation. And for this reason it matters little how logically correct it is to say that cognition ought not to be artistic, for with a non-artistic approach to knowledge we cannot fathom etheric reality. What matters is the nature of the world and not what cognition ought to be in principle according to certain logically correct assumptions. And so we have to say that an artistic moment arises when we raise ourselves from ordinary, object-based investigation to one that draws on Imagination.

And when we raise ourselves further to inspired cognition, the Inspirations we possess in our awareness will be of a kind that can be compared in turn to experiences of a similar and yet also dissimilar kind. These are moral experiences and the consideration of moral ideas. Inspirations from the world of spirit are similar to moral ideas by virtue of the fact that we are doing the same thing qualitatively when we experience inspired thoughts as when we entertain moral ideas and ideals in our awareness. Inspirations have a similar quality of inner experience to that of moral ideals, but are in turn completely different from them in that the moral ideal we formulate does not have the inward activity to realize itself through its own inherent strength. Our moral ideal is initially powerless in the world. We have to realize it through our physical personality, must place it into the world via our physical personality. The moral ideal as such remains a mere thought. This is not true of Inspiration. We accomplish this in a way that is qualitatively similar to moral ideas, moral impulses; but its participation in the world shows it to be something real, something powerful—something that acts as natural forces do. And thus we here immerse ourselves in a world that must be conceived as we conceive the world of morality, except that it is intrinsically real by virtue of its own strength.

And when we have progressed in Inspiration to the point where we now stand within a world of spirit and soul so that this world reveals content to us, something further is still required to fully experience this soul-spiritual world. We have to carry into this world of spirit and soul something that does not exist in our abstract world of thoughts. We have to carry into it devotion to the subject of enquiry. You see, we cannot fully know a being or force in the world of spirit and soul unless we can let our whole being pass over entirely, stream lovingly into what comes towards us through Inspiration. Inspiration is initially really only a revelation of spirit and soul. The inner nature of such revelation unveils itself to us when we ourselves, in loving devotion, pour ourselves out into what inspires us. And at this point, as we experience a living enhancement of spirit-soul reality, we enter upon Intuition.

That is intuitive perception. Shades of Intuition are already present of course in ordinary life, and they live in religious sensibility, in religious feeling. What is only inward in religious feeling, existing without us actually living in a distinctive world, becomes filled with reality in spiritual Intuition. And so spiritual Intuition is both similar to and very dissimilar from merely religious sensibility. Religious feeling on its own remains subjective. In spiritual Intuition our inner being streams into objectivity, lives amidst and within spirit-soul reality. And so we can say that the intuitive mode of supersensible cognition is both similar to and dissimilar from religious thinking.

If we therefore create a certain sequential progression in these stages of higher knowledge, we can say that we first have the object knowledge of ordinary life, a 'naturalistic' mode of cognition if you like. We then come to knowledge through Imagination, which is artistic, then to knowledge through Inspiration, which is moral, and then to knowledge through Intuition, which is religious in the sense I described. (Lecture in Dornach, 27 December 1921, GA 303, pp. 88–91.)

If we first rise to imaginative cognition, then to inspired cognition, what we can call 'standing outside things' becomes different in respect both of the external world and our inner nature.

In respect of the outer world, through imaginative cognition we first arrive at pictures. If we relate in the right way to these pictures they become images of what surrounds us as an external spiritual world. But now inspired cognition must play its part. Through Inspiration we gain knowledge of an external world of spirit that surrounds us as the outer sense world does with its colours, tones, currents of warmth and so on. If we now stand facing these spiritual surroundings we must always say that they are something other than we ourselves. We begin to discern elemental beings, the beings of higher hierarchies in these external spiritual surroundings: they are other than we are. In this process we increasingly become aware of ourselves as spiritual beings but we also learn to distinguish ourselves from beings that are different from us.

But as we practise the exercises that lead us to perceive this external spiritual world around us, we also make inner progress. And the discovery we first make in an inward direction is that we learn, as it were, to lower our estimation of our head with its store of knowledge. By contrast we ascribe increasing value to the form of knowledge that is more focused in the heart, if I can draw on the human organism here as reference. It is not so much a matter of the physical heart but of its etheric and astral aspects, of which we now become strongly aware. And now something of very great significance becomes very bright, illumined knowledge in us.

Look, I can describe what we can perceive here roughly in the following way. Let us imagine that this is the human heart here, and above the heart is everything that we value so greatly when we consider our life of thoughts on the physical plane. We also feel this weaving of thoughts in the head. If, before we develop higher cognition, we engage with our whole nature and being, we feel our thoughts to be an extraordinarily distinguished or let us say genteel aspect of ourselves. These thoughts of ours are not particularly concerned with our own personal concerns. Think of a triangle. We have to surrender to its laws without 'Lord Thought' worrying very much about whether I happen to have a headache at present or a stomach ache. He is entirely indifferent really to my personal mood, to whether I am happy, sad, in pain or feeling well. The idea of the triangle rules with a certain elegant nonchalance in my head consciousness and is little concerned with my subjective condition. This is why people who are only concerned with their subjective feelings fall asleep whenever one starts speaking of ideas that do not relate to their subjective state.

Well, yes, that is to some degree a refined and elegant world in which no attention is given to subjective feelings. But if a person mingles his subjectivity into this refined world, and feels close to his own being, this feeling passes through the heart, in a sense radiating downwards from the head to the rest of him; and at the same time something else rises from the rest of his being. What is it that rises up?

What rises up are feelings, instincts, drives, passions. All such impulses surge upwards. Here we have our being in a very subjective realm. And all that surges upwards of this kind also contains the bubbling organism itself. What boils and bubbles in the gut, in the stomach, or elsewhere in us, surges upwards with these drives and instincts and informs us. Up above, one can say, is the elegant and genteel world which does not, however, become soulful in us since it is unconcerned with the subjective element. It is ultimately of no concern whether Mr Smith entertains the idea of a triangle, of a lion, or whether Mr Miller does. Thoughts themselves are not concerned with the subjective element. Soul quality only arises when something springs from our inner being and imbues these thoughts with feelings or instincts. If Mr Miller is a hero for instance, and conceives the idea of the lion, then within him feelings pulse up from below that are tinged with fearlessness in the face of such a creature. Mr Smith, on the other hand, may be a coward, and the very thought of a lion might therefore make him tremble in fear. The subjective element enters in here, the quality of soul. The thought of the lion as such has a general, universal quality that is not soulful or inward: a spiritual quality. But what rises towards it from within us as drive or instinct colours it with soul quality. The idea of the lion acquires soul quality depending on whether Mr Miller immediately thinks of the weapon he will use to fight the lion with, to defend himself against it heroically, or whether Mr Smith immediately thinks of running away and hiding. In ordinary life this is what renders everything soulful. And this soul quality always in a sense shines up into the spiritual element.

But if you now progress to imaginative cognition and from there to inspired cognition, things become different. Here, to begin with, you will be faced with the great effort of repulsing the drives and instincts that surface, of preventing them coming to expression, since they will rise up in a much clearer because unvarnished way. They must be repulsed, not allowed to come to expression. But something else rises up as well. Rather than drives and instincts, a sum of thoughts rise through the heart—which in certain respects now becomes a wondrous sense organ, becomes as great as the whole blood organism, becomes a great etheric sense organ—towards the upper thoughts stimulated by the outer world, which dwell so genteelly in their palace there. These rising thoughts are in fact mighty pictures, and do not in any way express what otherwise surges up from the organism. Instead they express what we were before we were born.

We learn to perceive ourselves in the world of spirit before we were born on earth or conceived. This is what rises towards us. By virtue of what rises there we are not engulfed by our drives and desires but, in imaginative and inspired knowledge, are transposed into our existence in the world of spirit before we descended to physical embodiment. By learning to perceive ourselves in this existence, we learn at the same time to know through Imagination and Inspiration something other than our external spiritual surroundings, where we meet elemental beings, angels, archangels and so forth. We learn to know ourselves out of wisdom itself in our being expanded and enlarged beyond earthly existence.

But this offers us a very significant insight into soul experience. We gradually realize that this soul experience has streamed out entirely within our head and now dwells there. It has formed the head as its reflection; and this now presents itself to the outer world so that the latter can paint the pictures there which we receive and retain in our memory. But here below we have this life that does not [...] become so intensely bound up with the physical, that remains more detached from it. And by virtue of this we can look down into ourselves when the heart becomes the eye to look down on this aspect of us, look down into the flaming, singeing, burning emotions, desires, passions on the one hand and, on the other, on what may not unite with them, our eternal being that lives alongside all this.

And now it becomes clear to us that our soul relates to our head in so far as it is buried or interred in it—it rests within it. The head is really only an external organ of reflection for our physical surroundings. We only encompass the external world there. We encompass our own being when we look deeper into ourselves through the heart. Ordinary life only throws up the waves of emotion that rise within. But when we learn more through higher knowledge, our eternal existence rises up, and the soul learns to unite with the spirit that we are ourselves. The outer world we observe as spiritual surroundings is not us. What we now perceive within by looking through our heart as a kind of sense organ is we ourselves. The path that otherwise only leads us into the soul's outer aspects of drives and desires now leads us also into the eternal soul that exists within us, and that is permeated by spirit, that is as spiritual as our outer spiritual surroundings. And now we enter the realm where the soul is one with the spirit.

However much you look back to your brain, it is physical, and you yourself are physical. And the brain is of course also the chief province of modern materialistic psychology. People say they are studying the psyche, the soul, but in fact they are only studying the brain. That's possible since the brain is an expression of the soul, the soul is buried there: it is interred; the corpse of the soul rests there. This corpse of the soul is the domain of modern psychological enquiry. But the soul as such, its intrinsic nature, united with spirit, lies below the heart; and there it is only outwardly and not intimately connected with drives and desires.

But now we can make another discovery. You see, if you take some sense such as the eye and vision, at first you look around physically. Let's ignore the fact that we are usually in artificial light here. It is easy to prove that this too still has something to do with sunlight, albeit circuitously. But we'll overlook that for now. Let's just imagine a lovely morning in the open air, in sunshine out of doors rather than this terrible lighting. Let's imagine this. It does happen sometimes after all. Yes, we see the sunlight everywhere, since the sun is not only this disc or sphere but it shines. When it shines upon a flower, the rays are reflected back to us. The sun penetrates our eyes, and we therefore perceive the flower, and by means of this form the idea or picture of the flower. All objects become visible by virtue of the sun. That's easy for everyone to understand—that our capacity to see the objects around us is due to the sun conveying to us, via our head and eyes, everything that we know about the outward, physical properties of these objects. And yet the eyes do not only perceive the sun and sunlight. There is a deeper truth in the words in *Faust*:

> The sun sounds forth the ancient tune
> of brother spheres in rival song.[17]

Such universal harmony does exist, and what comes to expression of this harmony in our atmosphere is ultimately also a reflection of the sun, so that tone also originates in the sun and arrives here, albeit circuitously, from it. Everything perceptible in the external physical world comes from the sun: warmth, tone—everything, though not as directly as light does.

And now I have to say something that may appear surprising at first, that may seem hard to comprehend initially. But we can get to grips with it as long as we pursue it in the way we are used to pursuing things through anthroposophy. In what we see outwardly through the presence of the sun, and by our sensory involvement in the outer world that sunlight makes visible to us, we actually dwell within the solar element. We dwell within the external, physical-etheric solar element.

On developing imaginative cognition, and inspired cognition—if I can put it like that, although this has to be understood as I just described—and delving deeper into our own being by passing through the heart, this solar element changes. At a certain point, where inspired cognition arises, and where, with inspired knowledge, we are active in a real world of pictures, it seems to us as if, all of a sudden, in an inner, soul-spiritual jolt, we are sent headlong into the sun itself.

This is an experience whose importance you should reflect upon. This sun shines on us on earth. As human beings we perceive what surrounds us as reflection of solar qualities. But the moment we reach inspired cognition, where the heart becomes an organ of self-perception, as I described, we suddenly feel ourselves to be within the sun. We no longer feel as if we were looking upward to the sun taking its course through the heavens—I'm speaking only of its apparent motion—but, when our heart becomes our sense organ, we feel it to be within the sun and moving with it. Our experience is that the heart is carried away into the sun, the sun becoming the eye with which we now look at what begins to surround us, our ear too, and our organ of warmth perception. We now no longer have the feeling that we are outside the solar realm, but rather that we have moved into it, and now stand within light. We are always otherwise separate from the light. Now, having immersed our being in our heart, we have the sense of a world where we stand within the light, and our own being is light. With our light organs, which we now possess in the streaming, wafting light, we are in touch with spirit beings. Our soul now becomes related to the world that is not separate from the sun but is, rather, within it. And I'll say explicitly, we become linear, ray-like, feeling ourselves to be as if on the sun's path. And if higher knowledge now advances only a small step further, we not only feel ourselves to be within the sun but in a sense to have gone beyond it. Formerly we were a little person down below, and looked up to the sun. Now we have entered the sun and feel our soul being to be within it; and the world that previously surrounded us is within us. (Lecture in Dornach, 6 May 1922, GA 212, pp. 69–78.)

In relation to perceptions and insights that have a healing effect we feel that they unite us with the world of spirit: through them we are resolved into the spiritual world, becoming one with it, making our way to the gods, to our own immortal soul. We make our way to what we experience after passing through the portal of death and finding ourselves in the world of spirit; but we also make our way to what we experienced before we descended to the earth from the spiritual world through conception or birth. We feel all this as if we had offered up our existence to the world, but in consequence have become inwardly fuller and richer. Only by gradually becoming the world itself, as it were, do we encompass our own full human inwardness. And the way in which such knowledge, this healing knowledge, works its way into us, gives us the sense of how all human existence is dependent on our coming together with the world. Likewise we gradually come to feel that living without these healthy truths is like living our way into the world without organs to assimilate food, like being compelled to consume ourselves. And if we absorb what we feel must be rejected, this world content that makes us sick, it feels like consuming ourselves, and becoming ever more diminished.

That is the difference between seeking the truth in a merely intellectual way and penetrating to real spiritual insights [. . .]. In the intellectual domain we can dispute about idealism, spiritualism and materialism without any intense human participation beyond friendly discourse. But when we engage with spiritual truths, healthy, spiritual perceptions, materialistic ideas will start to pain us because we recognize that a person is consuming himself in these truths of a materialistic hue. Thus spiritual truths also acquire two nuances, which we can feel very sharply if we gradually live our way into spiritual perception. We learn to perceive the affinity of truth with love, the affinity of healthy perception with human selflessness—not the kind that loses the self but, by developing, comes properly into possession of self. When a person learns to go out of himself and enter into the world, and becomes selfless in this sense—not void of content but filled with world content—then this kind of selflessness leads him to true human existence, to true human feeling, to soul content altogether.

This surrendering to spiritual realities, which is similar to love, is what then impresses itself upon us as a kind of quality of character. It becomes a characteristic trait in someone who is able to take up spiritual insights. And therefore it is also true to say that we do not sense any great impulses of character arising from cultivation of a merely rational, intellectual outlook, because this does not touch so much on people's personality. But when we encompass the inmost core and reality of spiritual insight, we will also discover that we cannot acknowledge it without it changing our character, so that, to be paradoxical for a moment, it inscribes characteristics into our soul's flesh and blood: an inclination for selflessness, for love. This is what distinguishes the cultivation of spiritual truths from that of physical truths.

And in turn we learn to see how we consume ourselves inwardly, remain enclosed in ourselves if we absorb unhealthy insights—how we really do eat away at ourselves in a spiritual sense. We come to see what an inmost egoism in human nature can be, thus learning to perceive egoism on the one hand and love on the other as two nuances of feeling. We can even say that the effects of spiritual-scientific perception upon our character, and the need for them as we develop, are among its greatest fruits. Merely rational understanding and knowledge behave really like a plant root formed artificially of wax. No plant will grow from it; it has also been made by our powers of reason, artificially. All the knowledge so acclaimed today has been formed artificially through reason. But a real plant emerges from a real root. And from real perception and knowledge, by means of which we can unite our spirit with the spirits of the world, our whole inner being gradually emerges too: we become someone who has a vivid sense of what selflessness, selfless love, and what egoism are. And from this insight we now gain the impetus and momentum to be active in life in the right way, in selflessness; or, where necessary—for instance as preparation for life—drawing on our own resources and not glossing over anything but developing this egoism in full awareness.

By this means a certain clairvoyance arises in human self-observation, and in the realization of this self-observation in outward action. A soul-spiritual human being emerges from what spiritual perception and knowledge can become. And in consequence we approach the moral domain in an entirely practical and realistic way. (Lecture in The Hague, 16 November 1923, GA 231, pp. 38–40.)

7. Four Stages in Soul Development for a Thinking in Tune with Reality

All true knowledge that desires any prospect at all of engaging with the world's enigmas has to emerge from the seed of wonder. However acute a thinker may be—and he might even suffer, let us say, from excessive acuity—he will get nowhere if he has never passed through the stage of wonder. He may cleverly connect ideas, and nothing he undertakes in this way will be wrong, but just because it is correct does not mean it relates to reality. Before we embark on thinking, before ever setting our thoughts in motion, it is most necessary to have passed through the state of wonder. And thinking that is activated without this will really only remain a play of thoughts. Thinking must be rooted, if you like, in wonder.

[. . .] But after wonder another state of soul is needed, and this we can best describe as reverence for the subject of our reflections. After the state of wonder, that of reverence or veneration must come. Any thinking that emancipates itself from reverence, from looking up with reverence to the subject of reflection, will never succeed in penetrating reality. Thinking must never, as it were, perform its self-delighting pirouettes in the world. It must be rooted, once it has advanced beyond initial wonder, in a feeling of reverence for the foundations of the universe. [. . .]

But someone who has developed a certain degree of reverence in his feelings and then, since he has now experienced it, tries to advance further with merely ordinary thinking will also get nowhere, will find himself in an insubstantial realm. He would find his way to something right and, because he has progressed through the first two stages, this rightness would be pervaded by various well-founded perspectives; and yet he would soon inevitably find himself on uncertain ground, for a third stage has to establish itself in our soul after we have sufficiently experienced wonder and reverence. We can describe this third stage as 'feeling oneself in harmony with the laws of the world'. [...]

But this wise harmony with the world is not something we can easily establish without more ado. If it were that easy you would never now experience Lucifer's temptation, nor would anyone ever have done. You see, though what we mean when we speak of knowledge of good and evil, acquiring the fruit of the tree of knowledge, was certainly meant to happen for humanity, it was destined for a later time. Humankind sought to acquire the capacity to distinguish between good and evil at too early a period, and this must be seen as a flaw. Through Lucifer's temptation people sought to prematurely acquire something destined for a later time. And this could lead only to inadequate knowledge, which relates to the true knowledge humanity should have gained as a premature birth relates to a full-term birth. [...]

In turn it might seem strange to people today if, say, someone should tell them: 'You understand the theorem of Pythagoras fully, that the sum of the square on the two sides is equal to the square on the hypotenuse, or even something much simpler, that $3 \times 3 = 9$. But if you wish to understand its deeper, hidden meaning you must still pass through certain inner experiences.' And a modern person would laugh still more loudly if he were told he would only fully understand such matters if he brings himself into harmony with the world's laws, which have so ordered things that the laws of mathematics appear to us in a certain way. People today still commit the original sin, really, of believing that they can understand everything at any stage, without attending to the need to first undergo certain experiences to reach such understanding—to be inwardly sustained, first, by an awareness that all our strict views and judgements cannot attain anything in reality.

This belongs to the third condition that we must describe. However rigorous we are in our judgement, we can still always be mistaken. Right judgement can only arise when we have achieved a certain maturity, and can wait until the judgement falls into our lap. Rather than exerting ourselves to find the right verdict we should exert ourselves to become mature so that the judgement itself comes towards us, and then our judgement will have something to do with reality. However much someone exerts themselves to judge correctly, he can never be sure that such exertion will lead him to a reliable view. We will only practise right judgement if we do everything in our power to grow in maturity, and then as it were await right judgements from the revelations that stream towards us. Someone who forms quick and ready judgements will naturally think that a person who falls into the water and is dead on being pulled ashore has drowned. But if we have grown wise, mature, through life experience, we will know that general validity means nothing, and that in each individual instance we have to consider specific circumstances: that we must always let the facts themselves form our judgement. Life itself will confirm this time and time again.

Let's take another case. Someone says something which contradicts your own view. You may say that what the other says is false. You have formed a different view of the matter. Well, it's possible that both of you are wrong *and* right in certain respects. At this third stage of inner development, you will not think that people having different views is of decisive importance. It tells us nothing at all: we are only standing as it were on the pinhead of our own opinion. Someone who has grown wiser and more mature will hold back with his own judgement, doing so even when it seems to him that he might be right. He holds back by way of experiment, in an exploratory way. But let's imagine that someone tells you something today and then in two months time he says the opposite. You can exclude yourself entirely from the picture; you have nothing to do with either case. If you just let the two circumstances work upon you, there will be no need to contradict anyone, since these two statements contradict each other themselves. The judgement is formed here by the outer world, not by you. Only then does a wise person begin to judge. It is interesting that people will never understand how Goethe, for instance, undertook his scientific enquiries unless they form this conception of wisdom in which things themselves can judge. This is the reason for Goethe's interesting statement [...] that we should never really form judgements or hypotheses about outer phenomena but that these phenomena *are* the theories, that they themselves express their ideas if we become wise and mature enough to let them work on us in the right way. It is not a matter of, as it were, setting our shoulder to the soul's wheel and pushing hard to roll out the view we hold to be true. Instead we should make ourselves more mature, and let judgements fall into our lap from the facts themselves. Rather than setting up our thinking as judge and jury, our relationship to thinking must be one in which we form it into an instrument through which things can express themselves. This means being in harmony with the world.

Having passed through this third stage, thinking should still not try to stand entirely on its own feet since first of all comes what we can regard as the highest soul condition we must attain if we seek the truth. This is something we can describe with the word humility. Wonder, reverence, wise harmony with world phenomena, humility and surrender to the world's occurrences: these are the stages we must pass through, which must always accompany thinking and never abandon it—for otherwise thinking arrives only at what is correct and not what is true. (Lecture in Hannover, 27 December 1911, GA 134, pp. 21–7.)

We have [...] arrived at a consideration of the state of soul that we spoke of as humility and surrender, and which appeared to us, initially, as one of the highest conditions of soul we must attain if thinking, what we ordinarily call knowledge, is to enter into reality, have something to do with true reality—in other words, a thinking that has raised itself to states of soul where we first acquired wonder, then what we can call reverent devotion to the world of reality, and what we then call being in wise harmony with world phenomena. A thinking that cannot also raise itself to the region characterized as the condition of humility and surrender cannot yet attain reality. Now this faithful humility is something we can only acquire by repeatedly and energetically trying to recognize the inadequacy of mere thinking, and above and beyond this also engendering in ourselves with increasing intensity a mood of soul that has no expectation that our thinking can give us knowledge of the truth. We should only expect our thinking to educate us to begin with. It is extremely important to develop this mood within us: that our thinking educates us. You see, if you pursue this principle very practically, you will get beyond certain things, overcome them, in a very different way from how people usually think they should. (Lecture in Hannover, 28 December 1911, GA 134, p. 28.)

We only actually maintain ourselves in reality by virtue of the fact that our thinking does not intervene in this reality, that it is preserved from doing so. And so we can make mistake after mistake in our thinking. When we subsequently correct these mistakes, we have educated ourselves, have grown wiser, but have not thankfully caused devastating effects with these errors. If we can increasingly imbue ourselves with the moral force of such a thought, we arrive at a humility that ultimately brings us to a point where, at decisive moments in life, we do not use thinking to learn about outward things.

This sounds odd, doesn't it? It also sounds impossible to realize. Yet although we cannot accomplish this absolutely, we can do so in some respects. The way we are as human beings, we cannot entirely discard the habit of judging things around us. We feel compelled to form views [...] and this means we have to do something in daily life that does not in fact penetrate to the depths of reality. Yes, we have to make judgements, but through wise self-education we should view our judgements with caution rather than holding them to be true. We should continually endeavour to look over our own shoulder, as it were, and recognize that whenever we employ our intellect we are, basically, tapping around in the dark and can very easily be mistaken. This is hard for people who are sure they are right, and wouldn't know what to do if they doubted the views they attach to every occurrence. Many people consider it of the utmost importance to assert their view or feeling about things, their likes and dislikes, as if these are of vital importance. Yet these are habits we must shed if we wish to guide our soul towards reality. We need instead to develop an outlook that could be characterized roughly as follows. Well, my judging is part of who I am, and so I will go on forming views in so far as this is necessary in daily life. But it is not essential to my recognition of the truth. If I wish to discern the truth I will always look carefully over my shoulder and regard every view I form with a certain degree of doubt or caution.

But, you may ask, how can we come to any thought about truth if we are prevented from judging? Well, I did hint at this yesterday: we should let things themselves speak, develop an increasingly passive stance towards things and allow them to express themselves to us. A great deal would be avoided if, instead of judging all the time, we let things speak their secrets. Goethe exemplified this most wonderfully, and we can learn it from him. Whenever he embarked on his enquiries into truth, he forbade himself to judge, and sought

instead always to let things themselves express their secrets.
[...]

It is hard to discern the difference between judging and allowing reality to instruct us. But if we grasp it, and employ judgement only for practical purposes in daily life, allowing things themselves to teach us when we seek the truth, we can gradually develop a mood informed by humility. Humility is a state of soul in which we do not seek to discover the truth by our own efforts but instead await what reality reveals to us, what streams towards us from things; it is a state in which we can wait until we are ripe enough to receive such revelation. The faculty of judgement wants to find the truth at whatever stage a person has reached. Humility, on the other hand, does not seek to penetrate truths by force but instead works upon itself, educates itself, and calmly awaits the truth that will stream forth from things themselves towards us at a certain stage of maturity, and entirely penetrate us. The mood of humility works with a patience that seeks our own gradual advancement in wise self-education. (Lecture in Hannover, 28 December 1911, GA 134, pp. 31–4.)

We have seen from the whole tenor of our discussions so far that judgement does not in any way lead us into the world of reality but that we must, rather, educate thinking through wonder, reverence and so forth, and only by such means can we penetrate the real world. Then the sense world alters and becomes something entirely different. That is important: to approach this new element if we wish to discern the real nature of the sense world.

Let us assume that someone who has developed this soul

condition of humility to a high degree encounters a meadow in its full, fresh green. Initially he sees it as a general green since no flowers raise their heads above the grass. A person who has really developed the quality of humility to a high degree will gaze at this meadow and can do no other than feel something conjuring in him an inner mood of equilibrium. But this is an enlivened equilibrium, like a quiet, harmonious, even rippling of water. He will be unable to do anything other than conjure this picture before him. Likewise, with everything he tastes or smells, he will inevitably feel within him something like an inner quickening. No colour, no tone leaves him unaffected. Everything conveys something which elicits from him an inner, vibrant response: not the response of a judgement or opinion but one that originates in this inner quickening. In short, the whole sense world discloses itself to him as something he can call by no other name than 'will'. Everything in the sense world comes towards us as the sway of a streaming will. Please take special note of this: someone who has acquired the quality of humility to a high degree discovers will holding sway everywhere in the sense world. You will therefore understand that even someone who has only begun to develop this quality of humility will find it very unsettling if, let us say, he sees someone approaching him dressed in a 'fashionable clash' of colours. He simply cannot help having a lively inner response to everything around him. He will always be connected with the whole world through the will that he feels and experiences in everything. He approaches reality by virtue of the fact that he is bound up through will with the whole sense world. And in this way the sense world becomes for him like a sea of differentiated will. But in consequence, what we otherwise only feel to be spread out before us acquires a certain density. It is as if we are seeing behind the surface of things, listening beyond them, and hearing streaming will everywhere. If you have read Schopenhauer, let me say that he had a one-sided intimation of this presiding will, in the world of tones only. This is why he describes music in general as the differentiated workings of will. But in fact everything in the sense world lives in the sway of will for someone who has learned humility.

Once we have learned to sense will presiding everywhere in the sense world, we can then advance further, as it were penetrating through the sense world into the secrets concealed behind it which are otherwise removed from us.

To understand what should now come, we first have to ask how we know anything about the sense world at all. The answer is simple: through our senses. The ear tells us of the world of tones, the eye of the world of colours and forms, and so on. Our sense organs convey the sense world to us. In daily interaction with this sense world, we allow it to affect us, and we make judgements. Having developed humility, we let the sense world affect us, but then we feel also how the sway of will streams to us from things, how we swim with things, if you like, in a common ocean of presiding will. When we feel this sway of will from things, the momentum of our development carries us as if by itself to the next level. And here, having reached this quality of humility by passing through preceding stages—which we referred to as knowing ourselves to be in harmony with world wisdom, reverence and wonder—the interplay of these qualities with the last acquired, the quality of humility, makes it possible for us to grow together with things, to merge with them, through the etheric body which stands behind our physical body. In this presiding will we first grow together with our sense organs, that is, our physical body merges with things. When we see, hear, smell things, etc., this acts in such a way that, in humility, we feel as if the sway of will is streaming into us through our eye, we feel ourselves corresponding with things. But behind the physical eye is the eye's ether body, and likewise the ear's ether body underlies the ear. We are entirely permeated by our etheric body. In just the same way as the physical body can grow together with the things of the sense world through the sway of will, so the etheric body can grow together with things too. And as the etheric body merges with things, an entirely new manner of perception, or mode of vision, comes over us. The world is then changed to a much more pronounced degree than it is when we advance from sense appearance to the sway of will. When we grow together with things with our etheric body, the things of the world make an impression on us such that we cannot leave them as they are in our ideas and concepts, but instead they are changed for us as we come into relationship with them.

Think of a person who has cultivated the soul state of humility. Let us say that he looks at a green, sappy plant leaf, and turns his eye of soul upon it. He cannot simply leave it as it appears, this green, lush leaf, but at the moment he looks at it he feels that it has the potential to become something quite different. If you consider the green plant and its leaves, you know that it gradually grows taller, and that colourful flower petals emerge from it. The whole plant is, really, a transformed leaf. Goethe pointed to this already. Briefly, someone who looks at such a leaf will also see that it is not yet complete, that it seeks to grow beyond itself: he sees more than the green leaf before him. The green leaf affects him, touches him, so that he senses within him something like burgeoning life. But if he looks at dry tree bark, he grows together with it, by contrast, only through something like a mood of death. He sees *less* in the dry tree bark than its actual reality. Someone who only considers the bark's sensory appearance can admire it, take pleasure in it, and does not perceive the shrivelling, desiccating quality that can fill the soul with thoughts of death and decay.

There is nothing in the world which, when the ether body grows together with things, does not give rise to feelings either of growth, unfolding, sprouting, or instead of decay and decomposing. In this way we gain insights into phenomena. (Lecture in Hannover, 28 December 1911, GA 134, pp. 35–8.)

If we know ourselves fully, we usually cease to love ourselves. Self-love generally stops as we begin to know ourselves; and this self-love that is always present in people before they attain self-knowledge—for it is illusion to think that people don't love themselves, they do, more than anything in the world—is something we have to overcome. We must become able to let go of ourselves, overlook ourselves. As we develop inwardly we must learn to put the way we are at present to one side. We have already achieved much if we become humble. But we ought not to love ourselves at all. We must always be capable of feeling that we can push ourselves aside.

You see, if you can't set aside everything you love in yourself, all the errors, flaws, pettiness, prejudices, sympathies, antipathies and so on, then, as you develop, all this pettiness and prejudice will lead to forces getting mixed up with what must flow into you if you are to become clairvoyant. These forces will stream into your physical and etheric body and live there as flaws and destructive processes. As long as we are unconscious during sleep and cannot yet ascend into worlds of clairvoyance, the good gods protect us by preventing these forces streaming into our physical and etheric body with the currents flowing from the world of presiding will and presiding wisdom. But when we raise our consciousness into the world of clairvoyance, the gods no longer protect us, since the protection they afford consists in the very fact of rendering us unconscious. Then, instead, we ourselves must push aside all prejudices, sympathies, antipathies, and so on. We ourselves must eradicate this, for if we still retain self-love, desires that attach to our person, if we are still able to make judgements based on personal predilection, then all these things will injure the health of our physical and etheric body as we develop into higher worlds. (Lecture in Hannover, 28 December 1911, GA 134, pp. 43–4.)

Notes

Page references indicate German editions.

1. GA 119, Rudolf Steiner Press 1968.
2. One finds a similar formulation in Rudolf Steiner's essay 'At the Dawn of the Michael Age' (in *Anthroposophical Leading Thoughts*, GA 26), 1924, where he writes: 'Hearts begin to have thoughts.' In a work bearing this title, Karl-Martin Dietz explored the connection between heart thinking and the Michael Age (Stuttgart, second enlarged edition, 2005).
3. While *Theosophy* (1904, GA 9) and *Knowledge of the Higher Worlds* already contain exercises that can be assigned to different stages, they are not yet so clearly differentiated, and Steiner does not yet employ in them the terms Imagination, Inspiration and Intuition.
4. In the second edition of *Knowledge of the Higher Worlds*, in 1910, Rudolf Steiner added to the title of the chapter on these exercises the heading 'Development of the Etheric Body'. Cf. M.M. Sam, 'Zur Editionsgeschichte von "Wie erlangt man Erkenntnisse der höheren Welten?"', in *Beiträge zur Rudolf Steiner Gesamtausgabe*, no. 116/1996.
5. GA 10, in the chapter 'Some Effects of Initiation'.
6. Lecture in Berlin on 6 July 1915, GA 157, p. 298.
7. Lecture in Munich on 25 November 1912, GA 69a, p. 119.
8. The four exercises as described here correspond to the 'Probationary Path' described by Annie Besant in her book *Path of Discipleship* (first English edition 1899).
9. J.W. Goethe, *Faust II*, last verses.
10. 'What is suited, primarily, to making the head's rational and

logical thinking deeper and more inward starts quite simply. Our thinking thereby becomes free and independent of all sense impressions and experiences. We can say that it is concentrated *in a point* which we have entirely in our power. This creates an interim centre for the currents of the etheric body. This focal point is not yet in the heart region but in the head. The seer perceives it there as the starting point of movements.' (GA 10, p. 142.)

11. Final lines from Friedrich Rückert's poem 'Welt und Ich'.

12. Rudolf Steiner here originally used the theosophical expression 'chela'.

13. See lecture of 28 March 1910 in Vienna, in GA 119, pp. 195 ff.

14. See GA 13, pp. 309ff., 316 ff.

15. Named after the French physician, anatomist and anthropologist Paul Broca (1824–80) who located the speech centre in the brain.

16. See GA 253, lectures of 13–16 September 1915.

17. J.W. Goethe, *Faust I*, Prologue in Heaven.

Sources

The following volumes are cited in this book. Where relevant, published editions of equivalent English translations are given below the German titles.

The works of Rudolf Steiner are listed with the volume numbers of the complete works in German, the *Gesamtausgabe* (GA), as published by Rudolf Steiner Verlag, Dornach, Switzerland.

RSP = Rudolf Steiner Press, UK
AP / SB = Anthroposophic Press / SteinerBooks, USA

GA

10　*Wie erlangt man Erkenntnisse der höheren Welten?* (1993)
　　Knowledge of the Higher Worlds (RSP) / *How to Know Higher Worlds* (SB)

12　*Die Stufen der höheren Erkenntnis* (1993)
　　Stages of Higher Knowledge (AP)

13　*Die Geheimwissenschaft im Umriss* (1989)
　　Occult Science (RSP) / *An Outline of Esoteric Science* (SB)

25　*Kosmologie, Religion und Philosophie* (1999)
　　Cosmology, Religion and Philosophy (RSP / AP)

62　*Ergebnisse der Geistesforschung* (1988)

78　*Anthroposophie, ihre Erkenntniswurzeln und Lebensfrüchte* (1986)
　　Fruits of Anthroposophy (RSP)

84　*Was wollte das Goetheanum und was soll die Anthroposophie?* (1986)

88　*Über die astral Welt und das Devachan* (1999)

119　*Makrokosmos und Mikrokosmos* (1988)
　　Macrocosm and Microcosm (RSP)

253 *Probleme des Zusammenlebens in der Anthroposophischen Gesell-schaft* (1989)
    Community Life (AP)
303 *Die gesunde Entwickelung des Menschenwesens* (1987)
    Soul Economy and Waldorf Education (AP)
305 *Die geistig-seelischen Grundkräfte der Erziehungskunst* (1991)
    The Spiritual Ground of Education (AP)

All English-language titles are available via Rudolf Steiner Press, UK www.rudolfsteinerpress.com) or SteinerBooks, USA (www.steinerbooks.org)

Steiner

A NOTE FROM RUDOLF STEINER PRESS

We are an independent publisher and registered charity (non-profit organisation) dedicated to making available the work of Rudolf Steiner in English translation. We care a great deal about the content of our books and have hundreds of titles available – as printed books, ebooks and in audio formats.

As a publisher devoted to anthroposophy...

- We continually commission translations of previously unpublished works by Rudolf Steiner and invest in re-translating, editing and improving our editions.

- We are committed to making anthroposophy available to all by publishing introductory books as well as contemporary research.

- Our new print editions and ebooks are carefully checked and proofread for accuracy, and converted into all formats for all platforms.

- Our translations are officially authorised by Rudolf Steiner's estate in Dornach, Switzerland, to whom we pay royalties on sales, thus assisting their critical work.

So, look out for Rudolf Steiner Press as a mark of quality and support us today by buying our books, or contact us should you wish to sponsor specific titles or to support the charity with a gift or legacy.

office@rudolfsteinerpress.com
Join our e-mailing list at www.rudolfsteinerpress.com

RUDOLF STEINER PRESS